MW00781195

From Pain to Power

Kirk House Publishers
Burnsville, Minnesota

FROM PAIN
TO POWER

SEVEN STEPS TO
HEALTHY BOUNDARIES

ELLEN H. SAUL, MS, LP
LICENSED PSYCHOLOGIST

From Pain to Power: Seven Steps to Healthy Boundaries
© Copyright 2024 by Ellen H. Saul, MS, LP

All rights reserved. No part of this book may be used or reproduced in any manner whatsoever without the author's written permission except in the case of brief quotations embodied in critical articles and reviews.

The information in this book is distributed on an "as is" basis, without warranty. Although every precaution has been taken in the preparation of this work, neither the author nor the publisher shall have any liability to any person or entity with respect to any loss or damage caused or alleged to be caused directly or indirectly by the information contained in this book.

We have verified all website addresses as of January 1, 2024. Post-publication changes may occur.

This book is intended to provide helpful and informative material on the subject matter covered. It is sold with the understanding that the author and publisher are not engaged in rendering medical, health, psychological, or any other kind of personal professional services. If the reader requires personal medical, health, or other assistance or advice, a competent professional should be consulted. If you think you may have a medical emergency, call your doctor or 911 immediately. The author and publisher specifically disclaim all responsibility for any liability, loss, or risk, personal or otherwise, that is incurred as a consequence, directly or indirectly, of the use and application of any of the contents of this book.

First Printing: January 2024
First Edition

Paperback: 978-1-959681-39-7
eBook: 978-1-959681-40-3
Hardcover: 978-1-959681-41-0
LCCN: 2024900641

Cover art and design by Trina Brunk
Interior design by Ann Aubitz
Author photo by Sandra Julian
Photos by Ellen H. Saul, unless otherwise noted.

Published by Kirk House Publishers
1250 E 115th Street
Burnsville, MN 55337
kirkhousepublishers.com
612-781-2815

Visit the website for updates and PDFs of forms: https://www.ellensaul.com

ADVANCE PRAISE

From Pain to Power:
Seven Steps to Healthy Boundaries

"In *From Pain to Power: Seven Steps to Healthy Boundaries*, Ellen Saul gives us a profoundly effective roadmap for inner development to transform one's life. I highly recommend her real-world plan to discern and strengthen healthy boundaries, regaining Personal Power in the process. The authenticity of the experiences and the wisdom that shines from these pages will strike a chord with anyone who is struggling to move through or past a toxic relationship. A must-read."

~**Patricia Evans,** best-selling author of *The Verbally Abusive Relationship*

"Ellen Saul uses *her own experience* to give others careful, enthusiastic advice on how to move forward through difficult times. I hope *From Pain to Power: Seven Steps to Healthy Boundaries* receives the widespread response it deserves!"

~**Dr. Carl "Chuck" Lofy,** author of *A Grain of Wheat: Giving Voice to the Spirit of Change*

"This book has presented an accessible path to bringing awareness and liberation to the most challenging places in my life. I am grateful to Ellen for openly sharing her journey to wholeness as it inspires my own path forward. It is sure to be a gift to all who read it. Thank you, Ellen!"

~**Sarah F.,** enthusiastic client

"Thinking about your boundaries doesn't teach you specific steps to take to establish them. *From Pain to Power: Seven Steps to Healthy Boundaries* outlines those specific steps, rooted in your connection to your body and your inner knowing. Grab these skills, take these steps, set your new boundaries, and discover what can change in your relationships."

~**Hannah-Valeria Grishko,** Psychotherapist and Sandplay Therapist

"As a clinician, I look for resources that speak to the struggle my clients are expressing. Ellen's book is just that resource. She transforms setting boundaries into manageable steps that anyone can achieve."

~**Dr. Nancy Hawkins,** Licensed Psychologist, Shakopee Mdewakanton Sioux Community

"I grew up in a dysfunctional alcoholic family. *From Pain to Power* helped me learn to love my parts and meet their needs. It was a game changer. As you practice the seven steps, may you find wholeness and healing along with clarity about who you are."

~**Susan Kuske,** RN and Certified Healing Touch Practitioner and Instructor

"Ellen Saul's *From Pain to Power: Seven Steps to Healthy Boundaries*, crafted from real life experience and shared in accessible and readable language, beautifully integrates a lifetime of personal, family and clinical savvy. A reader can take whatever path inspires them the most—learning from the author's candid life stories, applying clear and doable exercises to one's life and, perhaps most importantly, gaining clarity on what boundaries are, and how to both create and honor them for oneself. This is a resource I will have multiple copies of in my office to share with patients. I found the book and practices shared within engaging to the mind, body and soul."

~**Laura Soble**, Licensed Psychotherapist, Sandplay Therapist, Jungian Analyst

TABLE OF CONTENTS

For all who need and deserve the safety of clear boundaries.

Season Turnings—Ellen H. Saul © 2021

INTRODUCTION TO THE SEVEN STEPS

I invite you to accompany me on an intimate journey through a major turning point in my life: betrayal and the divorce that followed. The pain that wove through that upheaval awakened me to the need for change in my moments and days. I yearned for a peaceful connection with myself, and for a sense of power and agency as I interacted with others. I groped my way forward through the weeks and months of separation, divorce, and its aftermath, using the steps which I later identified as the seven-step roadmap I'm sharing with you here. These steps for creating healthy boundaries allowed me to redefine myself, and to forge a new path forward in my life.

Each of us has our own turning points, and each of us can choose to become conscious of the boundaries we live within. *From Pain to Power: Seven Steps to Healthy Boundaries* offers a roadmap you can rely on wherever you are in your own journey of change.

This is my story. Not just a story of the day my life broke, but also one that includes key moments from both before and after that day. These moments shaped my boundary beliefs, the life rules I followed because I thought that was the only way to survive. Most of the time, I was unconscious of them. Using boundaries as a perspective on my journey helped me make sense of my history and change the direction in which I was going. During that process, I got clearer about boundaries and how they affect our lives.

What do I mean by boundaries? Often, we think of a boundary as the outside edges of a piece of property, such as the fence around the park, or how the skin creates the boundary of the physical body. In an interpersonal setting, boundaries often connote the ability to say no or to set limits for interactions.

I am also defining boundaries as the expression of the boundary beliefs you follow, consciously or unconsciously, as you go through your day, interacting with yourself and others. You may recognize them as "should" statements that run through your mind. Boundary beliefs may be as simple as "I should brush my teeth every morning," or as unconscious as physically shrinking away from conflict because your body is trying to stay safe. Boundary beliefs are the basis in our minds for actions we then take.

Peter Levine's groundbreaking development of a process called Somatic Experiencing has revealed the foundational importance of working with our bodies as we address the traumas that are stored there. During my separation and divorce, my activated body signaled me that healing work was needed, just as a painful foot can signal when there's a pebble in my shoe that I need to remove. I began to learn to be more attuned to my body's messages.

As I listened more carefully, I realized my body was a great signal system for letting me know when my boundaries were helping me, and when they were creating stress and misery. If I didn't notice when my gut was tight, or when I was holding my breath, I wouldn't recognize that my body was warning me, "Don't go here." Tuning into the messages and wisdom of my body has become a daily theme for me. I invite you to make your own somatic connections for awareness and power while we journey together through this book.

As I struggled to deal with the changes that came with divorce, I began to recognize various parts of me, or ego states, which responded in different ways to things that came up. You will meet some of these parts later on: for example, my inner child, the Screamer, my wise self, my adult self. Building positive relationships and boundaries with these ego states became a core concept of my work, both for myself and with my clients. When we give respect and affirmation to our various parts, we can repair wounds from the past, and tap into the energy, creativity, and qualities of each ego state. In addition, when we create clear boundary beliefs for and among these diverse parts, we also build an internal community of cooperation within ourselves.

Dr. Richard Schwartz developed Internal Family Systems Therapy (IFS) during the 1980s. He worked with some of the same concepts: that each of us has parts or subpersonalities which respond with different qualities and viewpoints. His structure acknowledges that each part has positive intentions and works to help us.

"All of us are born with many sub-minds—or parts," says Dr. Schwartz in *No Bad Parts: Healing Trauma & Restoring Wholeness with the Internal Family Systems Model.* "These parts are not imaginary or symbolic. They are individuals who exist as an internal family within us—and the key to health and happiness is to honor, understand, and love every part." (Schwartz, 2021)

I was determined to learn what would work better for me. As I dealt with separation—now a single parent of four children ages eight and under—I watched their father build a relationship with someone else, and I believed I would never smile again.

I felt stuck. I had no model for how to make something good out of this seeming failure. I felt shameful. I had no way to sort out my responsibility in this situation and didn't know what I could do to move forward. I didn't know how to support myself and I didn't have a circle of support.

I didn't realize then that my stuck feelings were connected to boundaries. I had learned these boundary beliefs through my experiences growing up. For example:

Be nice to everyone. Try to keep them happy all the time.

My boundary beliefs didn't provide any direction for responding to another person's lies, disrespect, or disregard for me when I said "Stop!" I felt helpless and afraid in the face of my husband's anger and broken promises. I held on to hope for the relationship when it was clear to others that the marriage was dying. All the while I was trying to figure out what was wrong with me, and what I had done wrong to cause all the pain that continued to envelop me.

Possibility on the other side of pain

Back then, I had no way of knowing how to get out of the chasm of pain, or the outcome of the journey I was about to begin. And I certainly had no way of imagining gifts would come to me during that journey. The gifts arrived, some sooner, some later.

I'm sitting here now, in my eighth decade. I am happy with my life. I have learned how to be compassionate with myself and gentle to my body, to listen to and delight in the younger parts of me. I have relationships that feed my spirit, including over thirty years in a second marriage which continues to blossom. I have work that deeply satisfies me. I continue to learn about myself, my body, my relationships, and my work. Creativity and joy are regular parts of my days.

Even if the place you are in feels utterly black, unknown, and hopeless; even if you feel confused and helpless right now, there is a path forward for you, too. I'm so glad you are here, reading *From Pain to Power: Seven Steps to Healthy Boundaries*. You will know how the steps fit for you. The roadmap for a new destination is here, available for you. And you can do it!

Why I am writing this book

One of the biggest changes I made post-divorce had to do with recognizing how unhappy I was with my life. I read Gail Sheehy's *Passages: Predictable Crises of Adult Life* (1977), and took the Life Satisfaction Quiz at the end of the book. Two major areas were highlighted as problems for me: I was not in a relationship, and I had no job outside my home. While I loved being a mom and raising my children, that at-home job did not satisfy all the parts of me, especially when all my kids were in school.

How does unhappiness connect with boundaries? When I thought about beliefs I held about my job as a mother, it sounded like this:

I should be the person who raises my children and that is my entire job in life.

Where did that boundary belief come from? I grew up with an at-home mom. That was my model. Without thinking about it or considering alternatives, I went into marriage holding a boundary belief that I, too, would stay home to raise my children.

I realized if I were to change the way I lived my life in response to the uninvited changes I was experiencing, I would have to create some new rules for myself, some new boundaries. For example:

I can be a good mom and have a career.

I thought about this a lot. The post-divorce budget was tight, but more than that, I could sense that I needed to find a direction for my life. If I did not, I would waste hours, days, and years, squandering time and using my energy in negative ways.

I began to ask myself the question, "What do I want to be when I grow up?" I was pushing forty at the time, but it is never too late to consider this.

The big question seemed to be this: What could I do that would use all my capabilities, and would be truly satisfying? I heard Dr. Chuck Lofy speak about Joseph Campbell's idea of

"The Hero's Journey." Here's a diagram that shows what the Hero's Journey looks like:

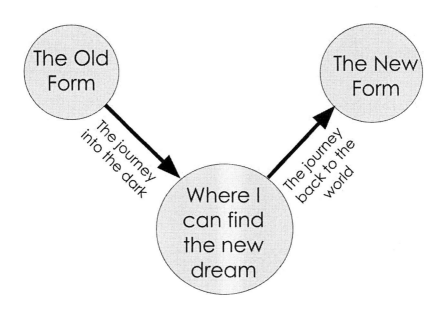

The Hero's Journey

The forms mentioned here are the structures that show up in your life. You already have a number of forms: your family or relationship roles; your health; your spiritual life or religious practice; whether or not you acknowledge feelings; your home, work, or school life.

For many reasons, a current form may change, quickly becoming an old form: death or divorce; a job change; a new spiritual practice or church; or beginning therapy. At times, the change arises from within, because you become aware that the old form—a manifestation of your heart's previous desires—no longer fits for you. Sometimes outside circumstances create change without your choice. When I first saw this diagram, I had already lost the form of "wife."

When I no longer fit the old form, I found myself on the "journey into the dark," in search of something new. That journey was often scary and difficult. Many times when I found myself in that dark place, I tried to sidestep difficult emotions and the sense of being in limbo by using my favorite list of avoidance activities to prevent discomfort. You might be familiar with common attempts to numb one's feelings by using food, alcohol, drugs, busyness, spending, relationships, computer games, or moodiness.

As I worked to stay present with my feelings—even when they were uncomfortable—I began to notice interesting signposts that pointed me toward possible future forms. Working with the concept of the Hero's Journey, I began to envision a path of my own.

I looked for a life direction that would satisfy me, and I gradually came to realize I wanted to help people as a psychotherapist. My new dream began to take shape. I interviewed Dr. Lofy, and he laid out some possibilities for me. I left his office, drove to the local college, signed up for a class and attended the first class, all on the same day. That was the start of my professional path. Step by step, as I worked with this process, new forms took shape: re-singled person, survivor, student, counselor, psychologist, spiritual person, speaker, partner, and later on, wife and stepmom.

Three and a half years after signing up for that first class, I had a master's degree in Community Counseling and a counseling job at a mental health agency. Two years after that I was licensed as a psychologist.

Today I have over thirty years of experience working with children and adults on all sorts of issues: trauma, depression, anxiety, relationship issues, and abuse. Along the way I have learned from my clients, and we have worked together to discover what's needed to help them.

In addition to my professional work, I have followed a parallel path of pursuing an education in myself. I have been learning about the parts of me, their boundaries, and how to be a good enough parent to them. I'm learning to notice my body's signals when I am getting upset. Learning what to do to return my body to a state of calm. Recognizing where automatic patterns from my childhood may not be the best solution. (Eating a 2 lb. bag of peanut M&Ms, for instance.) Learning to substitute an alternative action like going outdoors and taking three stunning photos. I have practiced effective new thoughts, new actions, and new words repeatedly, until they have become automatic. They feel so much better than the old responses. Each of these changes reflect the new boundary beliefs I have established to transform my life.

The inner work I have done has made me a better therapist. Issues that I had not yet examined left me blind to those issues in my clients. I learned about verbal abuse: where I had experienced it, how it affected me, and how I could respond effectively instead of crumpling inside. As I got a handle on it for myself, I began to recognize verbal abuse in the stories my clients shared with me, and could lead the way in helping them make changes.

Before my divorce, my idea of abuse was limited to physical assault. If someone had asked me, "Have you experienced abuse in your marriage?" I'm sure I would have answered, "No." I needed other questions to bring out what my body knew, but I avoided knowing consciously.

- Do you sometimes feel anxious about how your partner is going to respond to what you say?
- Do you sometimes censor yourself because you are worried about the response you will get?
- Does your body/your gut feel calmer and more peaceful when you are with your partner, or when you are away from your partner?

Then there was all the baggage I carried with me from my childhood, the boundary beliefs I operated by, even though I wasn't conscious of them. For example:

- It's not okay (read: not safe emotionally) to tell people what I'm thinking.
- It's not okay to want things or ask for them.
- It's not okay to ask questions or ask for help.

I wasn't even aware these were my rules for myself. I did know something wasn't working well in my marriage, but it took me a while to learn how my boundary beliefs impacted all of my relationships.

I have been able to make changes that have helped me in my life. I have had the privilege of counseling clients and supporting them in making some of the same changes. It is my hope that I can share the seven steps to building healthy boundaries with you, so you can benefit as well.

What might you get from this book?

Reading *From Pain to Power: Seven Steps to Healthy Boundaries* will give you information about boundaries and how they are already either helpful or unhelpful parts of your life. Completing the related exercises can give you experience and grow your skills as you work with your boundaries. You may also discover that some intangible gifts will show up in your life.

You can use this process to establish the healthy boundaries that you may not have acquired yet. As I share parts of my own story, and you consider your own, you might discover that you, too, do not have to remain in your pain.

Possibilities will open up. You can learn now what you didn't have the opportunity to learn early on. You can become a better parent to yourself than your parents might have known how to be to you when you were young.

You could come away with some understanding of the connection between boundaries and safety and your body. If ineffective boundaries might lead to loss of safety for you and for the people you care about, would effective boundaries seem more important? If there is a cliff, it helps to have a fence to keep folks from falling off. How do you recognize the cliffs in your relationships, and how do you create safety fences for them?

Here is a chance to explore why it might be important to be well-connected to your body and your spirit in order to have effective boundaries. Remember learning about a hot stove as a child? The feel of the heat lets your body know it isn't safe to put your hand on the stove. The same thing holds true for the ways our bodies give us warnings of emotional danger. Our stomach tightens up, our heart speeds up, our breathing becomes shallow and constricted.

If you have grown up with trauma, you may have learned to disregard these signals from your body because you were little and there was nothing you could do but wait it out, hoping you would survive. How can you know there's something to be alert for if you have learned to disregard your body's signals?

Another benefit of reading *Seven Steps to Healthy Boundaries* will be learning how to connect in a deeper, heartfelt way with your child self. You can learn how to repair the early wounds you may have experienced growing up. Your parents don't even need to suddenly start doing things differently. This is between you and yourself.

When you listen and respond to yourself on a regular basis, it lays the groundwork for changes in your relationships. Boundaries start with your connection to your body and your child self. From there you can expand these boundaries to interactions with other people in your life. You can be in charge of how you carry out your part of boundaries, as you pay attention to your own safety. It's amazing how the ripple effect works. The path that you choose allows you to move ahead in your life, regardless of the decisions or behavior of others.

It is my intention that this book will offer you hope, give you tools, and inspire you to borrow from the energy I have gained in this process. Make this process your own, use what speaks to you, practice the heck out of the skills you are learning, and you can change your life!

How I have organized this book

Each of the seven steps will have its own chapter, including a story illustrating the step, some thoughts about the step, and how each step relates to boundaries. There will be lots of examples, followed by Exercises for Change, where you can develop the skills to move ahead on your journey. Then you will encounter questions for reflecting on the experience you had doing the exercise, as well as some possibilities for your future self as you integrate new practices with your daily life.

How to use this book

You may choose to read this book for the story of my turning point and the journey that followed. When I was in the midst of my divorce, it was a huge relief for me to hear other people's stories and realize that I was not the only one struggling to deal with difficult feelings and challenges. They are universal, regardless of the specifics of your turning point experience.

You may also choose to do the exercises. They might be easy or difficult, reassuring or scary. If you do them, you will learn how to give yourself repair experiences. This is one way to heal old wounds and begin the process of creating new brain pathways and new outcomes for yourself. If you do the exercises and reflect on what each experience is like, a different part of your brain will light up, and you will have that experience in your body forever. This is quite different from reading about an exercise and then trying to remember it.

Do you want to get out of the pain and craziness? According to an unknown wise person, "Insanity is doing the same thing over and over and expecting a different result." These exercises hold keys to doing something different and getting a different result. You get to choose. You will know what resonates most for you. Your best self will take notice when you come across something that you need in the Seven Steps roadmap:

- Something that fills an empty space inside you
- A skill
- A thought or belief
- An experience

Feel free to tailor these exercise experiences so they fit for you. Right now, it may be enough just to read the rest of this book.

What I hope for you

So here we are. Wherever you are right now in your journey, there is a part of you that knows your life needs clear boundaries. *From Pain to Power: Seven Steps to Healthy Boundaries* is a roadmap that has worked for me, and it has worked for many of my clients over the past thirty years. Here's an example of moving through the Seven Steps:

Pain, you've got my attention.
>(Step One: Recognize your pain)

I'm finding help.
>(Step Two: Get some help for support and change)

It's okay to get help. I deserve it. That's my boundary.
>(Step Three: Identify your current boundary beliefs)

That feels good. I'll keep that one.
>(Step Four: Assess your boundary beliefs and keep or update)

It's still okay to get help, especially when it's hard.
>(Step Five: Create and practice effective new boundary beliefs)

"Can you give me a hand? Can I help you out?"
>(Step Six: Practice your new boundary beliefs with others)

Cheers! We're clear and connected. We're doing it!
>(Step Seven: Celebrate your changes and yourself)

I want you to know your power lies within you. You are making choices for yourself every day. My hope for you is that you choose to take the best care you can of yourself by creating the boundaries that will support you. As you go through the process I share with you here, you can learn to become wonderfully attuned to the amazing person you are and have always been.

I have complete confidence that you can learn to listen and respond to all the parts of you. I believe you will be able to give yourself repair experiences with clear boundaries that keep you safe. I wish for you a life where you have the joy of being closely connected to yourself every day. You can do it! I am cheering for you!

Cracked Earth—Ellen H. Saul © 2023

STEP ONE

Recognize your pain

This first step may not seem like an action step, but it is. You already know you're in pain, right? That's probably why you are looking at this book. There's the emotional pain of sadness, loneliness, or betrayal. Physical pain gets our attention when it shows up in our bodies. Our spirits are in pain when we are discounted, put down, or bullied. Even our minds can experience pain or distress when our thinking is confused, frustrated, or unsettled. We're aiming at recognizing the full range of pain.

Think back for a moment. When did you first start feeling the pain that you are experiencing? Did this pain convey a clear call to action to you? Or did it just register, and then you soldiered on? It's helpful to notice the signals our bodies give us when pain in any of its forms is present. A body signal lets us know some kind of change or action is in order.

Example: *I'm feeling kind of antsy now. What is my body telling me?*

Step One is about choosing to tune into yourself by respecting your body, its knowledge, and what it is asking from you. This may be easy to do once you decide it's important. Or, you may come up against a lot of resistance to becoming more attuned to yourself. Maybe it was safer for you as a child not to notice and speak up about what wasn't working for you in your family. The exercises at the end of the chapter can help you sort this out and proceed safely.

Let's begin with a story.

The Night My Life Broke Open

I went to sleep wearing a sexy black nightgown, yearning for my husband to notice and respond to me when he came home from working late. I had put the kids to bed and turned in early myself. At about 10:00 pm Neal arrived home. The noise he made coming in woke me and I sprang out of bed. Something was wrong. "What are you wearing?" he demanded. I had forgotten about the sexy nightgown. I stayed silent.

"I've been seeing Dawn," Neal said. "I was at her house tonight and her husband came home early. I left out the back door as he came in the front door."

Then the doorbell rang. It was Dawn's husband, wanting to talk. Somehow Dawn was called to come over, too. We all sat down around the kitchen table. Neal said, "We can break up two families, or we can all go home and work things out." Dawn agreed, replying "Whatever he says." Shortly after that, she and her husband left to go home.

Neal went on to say that he hadn't planned to tell me about the affair until he was quite sure Dawn's husband would tell me. He confessed that he had started seeing Dawn six months earlier.

Suddenly things began adding up:

- Neal had encouraged me to join the local city orchestra. His parents would babysit when I went to rehearsal one evening a week in case he got called in to the hospital for a delivery. (He was an Obstetrician/Gynecologist.)
- A friend of mine told me Neal had been seen at a local park with Dawn. I had ignored the comment.
- Another friend had asked me for advice: Should she tell a friend that the friend's husband was having an affair? It never occurred to me that she was referring to me.
- Neal gave me a very lovely opal necklace after I had been out of town for a few days for a cousin's wedding. There was no occasion for the gift.
- One evening I discovered Neal was not where he said he would be. Then he acted like everything was legitimate when my gut knew it wasn't.
- I found myself not believing my own gut's information and feeling more and more unsettled.

Neal moved out and went to stay with his parents in town. His mom cooked for him and did his laundry. It seemed to me that he had it way too easy. How was he going to figure out he wanted to come back if it was all cushy for him? Later he rented his own apartment. As they say, be careful what you wish for. When he had his own apartment I never knew where he was or who he was with.

I was a mess. I was providing daycare for the three children of a friend. I had to get up in the morning to make breakfast for my four children and get two of them ready for school before the daycare children arrived. After breakfast I would get the kids focused on an activity, and then retreat to the bathroom to cry. Then it would be time for the next round of childcare. Some days I couldn't manage to get dressed until afternoon.

During the evenings, there was the routine of supper, pajamas, stories, songs, and prayers. After the kids were in bed, I would call a friend or one of my sisters and spew out my pain and anger. Then I would call someone else. Then a third person. It was days before I could bring myself to tell my parents what was happening.

Neal and I started counseling. Nothing was happening. One day in our session I asked him, "Do you want our relationship?" His silence gave me his answer.

Christmas was weird. Neal came over when our kids were opening gifts. I had bought a gift for the kids to give him. There was no gift for me. Later, I heard that he had given Dawn an expensive camera.

Here and there, the kids and I began to find a new rhythm for our lives. I began to realize there was more peace in the house with Neal gone. But that wasn't what I wanted. I had achingly lonely times when the kids were with him for a weekend. They had experiences without me and met people I didn't know.

My frustration grew. I wondered to myself, "How can I make Neal see what he's losing? Maybe I should file for divorce." I talked this over with a friend. She asked, "Is that what you really want?" Of course, it wasn't, but I thought maybe it would shake him up and make him realize what he was about to lose. Then it hit me. If I filed for divorce, he would never have to take responsibility for his choice to leave our marriage. He could just shrug and say, "She wanted it." So I didn't file.

In January, Neal came over and let me know he had filed for divorce. As he told the kids, I sat there feeling like I was watching a scene from a movie. Realizing that I was powerless to stop what was happening was so hard. I tried to shut it out of my mind.

Negotiating the divorce was awful. How did I think we were going to manage that when we couldn't work out our marriage? As Neal and I sat at the dining room table talking things out, our youngest child, age two, came in with a question. Neal yelled at her to leave. She began to cry and ran from the room.

I was overwhelmed. I didn't have a job; I was going to have to manage on child support and maintenance payments. What amount would be enough for the kids and me to live on? I had to answer that question and many others that his lawyer asked.

Finally, I got a call letting me know that the papers were ready, and I should pick them up. Driving home, I pulled out into the side of an oncoming car. I realized then how vulnerable I was. I couldn't even drive safely. I went back to therapy.

What was going on with me:
- Crying a lot, but not when the kids could hear.
- Trying to keep things going, but not having much energy. Staying in my pajamas all day.
- Brain fog. Couldn't remember things. Not able to get out of the black hole.
- Obsessive thoughts. What was Neal doing? What was the other woman doing? How could I have been so stupid as to not know they had gotten together? When my gut told me something was wrong, how could I have blown it off?
- Mind racing all the time. Couldn't sleep. Cold all the time.
- I shut down. I felt disconnected.
- I felt ashamed. No one else in my family had been divorced.
- I only knew one person who was divorced. People didn't understand what I was going through.
- Dumped quietly by our couple friends. I was lonely. Living out in the country with lots of snow and few neighbors.
- Feeling helpless and a bit crazy. Believing I would never laugh again.

- I wasn't paying attention to my body or what was going on around me. I slipped on some ice, fell, and cut myself. I needed stitches.
- I felt alone. The person I thought would be my life-long partner had quit me.
- I had to pick up the pieces. I just didn't know if I could ever put them together again.
- I had no name for what I was going through. Now I know it's called depression.

Note: If this sounds familiar, now is the time to get some professional help. When emotions are this intense and affect your life to this degree, you need support to get through to the other side. Call 1-800-273-TALK (8255) to reach a 24-hour crisis center, or text "HOME" to 741741 for the Crisis Text Line, which serves people across the United States experiencing any type of crisis. It provides free, 24/7 emotional support and information through texting with a live, trained specialist.

If you are in physical danger, don't stay in the place where you are exposed to that threat. Get to safety. Get help. Here is the National Domestic Violence Hotline number: 1–800–799–SAFE (7233). If you worry about safety and keep hoping things will be okay, this book could be useful in helping you figure out how to make safety a reality for you and for the important people in your life.

Depression can change your thinking so dramatically that you believe your depressed state is pervasive, permanent, and personal. Pervasive: "Everything in my life is awful." Permanent: "It's always going to be like this." Personal: "It's all my fault."

Those beliefs aren't true. Remember that I thought that I would never laugh again? That was the effect of depression on my thinking.

Depression can be treated. Left untreated, it can lead to suicidal thoughts and actions. If you wonder about your level of depression, you could go online, take the PHQ-9, and get your score at https://psychology-tools.com/test/phq-9.

Then take steps to take care of yourself. These might include some or all of the following:

- Find a therapist and talk about how you are feeling.
- Learn some new thinking skills.
- Ask your doctor about medication for depression.
- Check with your doctor about your levels of vitamins and minerals.
- Choose to spend more time outdoors, moving your body.
- Make sure you are sleeping well.
- Look into how food affects your mood and consider some dietary changes.
- Find others who are dealing effectively with similar issues and join a group.
- Use the exercises in *Seven Steps to Boundaries* to improve your skills in emotional regulation, stress tolerance, interpersonal communication, and mindfulness.

Getting your mood stabilized can give you a foundation to address other issues you may be experiencing, such as grief, trauma, or going through a life transition.

> How would I get through the coming days and months? I couldn't stop the divorce my husband was choosing. I circled around the hope that I could change this outcome. I kept coming up empty.
>
> It wasn't until months later, as I got some counseling, that I began to learn how to do things differently. I started to learn that how I talk to myself matters. Discounting my needs, putting myself down, and blaming myself led to my feeling ashamed and depressed. All of that created negative feelings in my body such as muscle tension, stomachaches, and headaches. My body knew my negativity wasn't helping.
>
> The divorce was final in early June. The marriage was over. However, I was beginning to realize there was a lot of work ahead of me. Dealing with my feelings; figuring out how to live in the same town with Neal, his parents, and his girlfriend; managing school conferences; dealing with the local gossip and the huge amount of shame that whirled around inside me. I didn't yet realize how all these difficulties were connected to my boundary beliefs.

I wish I had known then that a year later I would be able to look back and see how I had changed. In the midst of everything that had gone on, all of which I had no control over at that time,

I chose to make changes that empowered me and gave me new strength.

Becoming aware of your body and your boundaries

What does any of this have to do with boundaries? For ten years, I had lived by boundary beliefs that seemed appropriate to me as a wife:

- *Be supportive and helpful.*
- *Don't ask anything for myself.*
- *Do not say "No" or "Stop."*

I thought I couldn't fulfill the "wife" expectations if I listened to my body's information. I struggled to read my body's signals. I knew about my sadness, the tears behind my eyes so much of the time. I couldn't have named my anger, but sometimes in the car alone, I screamed. I didn't identify my body's shrinking feelings and desire to hide from my community as shame.

My focus was outside me. Even after the divorce, I desperately wanted to create a different outcome with Neal. I had no idea I was trying to accomplish something I had no control over. I didn't have any sense of my boundaries. I couldn't tell where I stopped, and he began.

I didn't want to continue feeling so miserable. I had to find a new way to do things. I needed a solid foundation to move forward. I decided I would no longer depend on a relationship with someone in order to have a life and find joy.

I'm guessing that some of you reading this have experienced something similar in your lives. I was learning that if my mind and spirit were going to be joyful, my body had to be part of the plan. Getting reacquainted with my body's signals was one of the first steps I had to take to begin to have some boundaries that could serve me better.

Awareness of your pain

Why is it important to notice our pain? What can it teach us that we desperately need to learn?

The awareness-building stage of this process is especially important. When Neal decided to leave our marriage, I was VERY aware of my pain. What I wasn't aware of was all the ways in which I had been ignoring my pain for years.

I was also unaware of the disconnection that occurred inside me every time I believed the negative statements that I was hearing about myself, or took on guilt for things I didn't do. That was painful, but I did my best to ignore it. Of course, that's something I had learned to do as a child. My family wasn't comfortable with talking about feelings—in particular, difficult feelings. We didn't know how to be with each other until the feelings calmed and we were settled.

So why would it be important to know if I'm in pain? I don't want to feel pain. It doesn't feel good to be hurting. We are wired to move away from pain. Remember learning as a little kid not to touch a hot stove? That's how we stay safe and keep our bodies healthy. Pain can take many forms. We are going to look at distinct types of pain and how they show up in our lives: physical pain, intellectual or mental pain, emotional pain, and spiritual or energetic pain.

Each of these manifestations of pain provide you with an important message: something needs to change. Your body, your mind, your heart, and your soul are working hard to get your attention.

Imagine you are taking a walk, and your foot starts hurting. You realize there's something in your shoe that doesn't belong there. You have a choice to make. If you keep walking and put up with the pain, your foot will hurt more. If you stop and take out the pebble, or smooth out the wrinkle in your sock, your foot can return to a state of comfort. Your body is doing what it is designed to do well: send you louder and louder signals when something is amiss, so a small problem doesn't become larger and larger, causing you injury.

If your body is saying things aren't okay, are you paying attention? Will you take action to keep yourself safe?

Many of us were taught NOT to listen to our bodies. You may have gotten messages as you grew up that other people knew what was best for you. I went through a lot of years believing others' opinions about me and disregarding what I knew about myself. That's where I was when my life turned upside down.

Physical pain

Sometimes it's your body that first gives you the warning signal that all is not well. Looking back on ten years of marriage, my body gave me lots of signals that my safety was in question.

My stomach got tight whenever Neal raised his voice. I just wanted to run out of the room when I looked at him and saw disgust in his eyes. My breathing would catch when one of the kids did something and a sharp reply would come from Neal. There were times I felt frozen in place, wordless, unable to act to protect my kids, or to speak up in my own defense. And sometimes my upset would land on my kids because I didn't have the words to say "Cut it out!" or "No!" to Neal.

I hadn't learned that when my body was giving me a signal, my job was to take some action in response. Growing up, other people told me how it was for me, instead of asking me. The rules inside me, my boundary beliefs, were specific:

- *Pay attention to other's opinions.*
- *Turn off all the inside information.*
- *Don't act.*

These seemed to be the rules that worked out best for me. I continued to use them, more unconsciously than not, into adulthood.

Emotional pain, including depression, grief, rage, loneliness, sadness

My history of emotional pain and how I handled it goes back to early in my life. My mother had experienced several major losses by the time I was a toddler: her dad's death when she was 16, the death of her first child at 5 days old, and a miscarriage when I was just over a year old. These were stories I learned about much later.

My mother experienced depression in response. Though it was never named in our family, it had a powerful impact on me. Part of my energy as a child went into trying to help my mother feel better.

As she struggled in silence to recover from the loss of her pregnancy, Toddler Me wasn't getting the connection and emotional interaction I wanted and needed from her. I found some ways to fill that empty space. I began visiting our neighbors by the time I was four, ringing doorbells to find someone who would talk to me.

I believe I was about five when I helped an adult complete a task and received appreciation, delight, and warm fuzzies from them. On some level, I came to believe that if I helped someone, I might get recognition and warmth from that other person.

I also discovered that eating sweet things helped me feel better. I would sneak ice cream from the freezer when I woke up early on Saturday mornings. I stole candy from the corner drugstore for a couple of years when I was 7 and 8 years old.

These strategies helped me avoid feeling lonely, sad, or upset. When Neal moved out, the level of emotional pain I was feeling was overwhelming. Depression rolled in like a black fog. Like my mother, I couldn't name it. I fell back on my early strategies, since I hadn't yet learned new, more effective ways to cope.

There were moments when I felt rage like I had never felt it before. The size of the betrayal I was experiencing brought fantasies of taking a big sledgehammer to my husband's truck. I didn't. But part of me thought that would be really satisfying.

I felt bewildered a lot of the time. This situation had never been on my radar. I not only believed that people *should* keep their promises, but that other people—my husband in particular—*would* keep his promises to me. And now he hadn't. My world had rocked on its axis. I found it awfully hard to acknowledge what had happened without reexperiencing my feelings of betrayal.

I remember being overwhelmed with sadness multiple times a day after Neal moved out. Remember my pattern? Take care of the next needs of my children, shut myself in the bathroom and weep, then pull myself together, wash my face, and do the next round of childcare, while in the middle of the ongoing ache of depression.

My body was letting me know that things were off. It was trying to help me take care of myself and stay safe. However, I had learned early in my life that in my family it worked best for me to disregard my internal alarm system. The turning point of my divorce turned out to be a perfect time for me to get some help to learn how to get that alarm system working again. The exercises later in this chapter will increase your skill in receiving and using the help your body is trying to give you.

Intellectual or mental pain

No sooner had my husband told me that he was having an affair than my brain began to whirl. "How could he have done this? Why didn't I realize it? What is it in me that would pick a husband who would cheat on me? What's going to happen? Can this marriage be saved? What can I do? How can I get him to love me again? Did he ever love me? Is anything he ever told me true?"

And on and on. Not only were there all those questions, but my internal critic was cruel. "You idiot. You should have seen this coming. It must be your fault. You aren't enough for him.

You're not sexy or beautiful enough. You should have done more. You should have figured out what he wanted."

My thoughts kept going around in circles without stopping. Negative beliefs about myself were compounding. I was putting myself down and judging myself for what I believed was my failure.

I couldn't even say to myself, "Hey, cut it out. It takes two to tango. You didn't *make* him do this; he chose to do it." And I was far, far away from what I would realize later, that there are gifts in everything that comes to us in our lives. Even if it takes time for us to recognize them.

Mental pain counts. What does it feel like living inside your mind these days? Are your thoughts calm or chaotic? Can you feel some gratitude, or do you get caught up in judgments and frustration? Do you choose what you are saying to yourself, or do your negative thoughts recycle all on their own? How are you talking to yourself—gently and with compassion, or by yelling and putting yourself down? Once you recognize when it's not feeling good, you have taken the first step to making positive changes.

Spiritual or energy pain

When my husband told me about his affair, my spiritual beliefs took a hit. I asked, "Why is this happening, God? This can't be what *you* want. Please, change this!" I felt so alone. Had God abandoned me? I went to my pastor, hoping for some support, but I came away feeling emptier than before.

When my husband moved out, I kept praying that things would change, that he would change, and come back to our marriage. He chose divorce. I couldn't see how this was anything but wrong. My prayers were answered with something quite different from my ideas of how my life should be.

Notice for a moment: How is your spirit feeling these days? Bowed down and heavy, or looking up and seeing some breaks in the clouds? Feeling like you are on track, or carrying a heaviness that's connected with being off the mark? If you have a sense of a spiritual connection, is that feeling strong and supportive, or are your spiritual resources feeling weak and far away? How is your energy level? Low energy can be one of the ways your body is trying to let you know that things are just not right.

Sometimes, feeling completely miserable brings the awareness that you've been feeling bad for quite a while. You're just now realizing it. It's time for the first exercises to help you get back in balance, aware and prepared for action.

Exercises for Change: Working with your parts to identify your pain

These journaling exercises will provide you with repair experiences for all the times the big people in your life didn't know how to be attuned to you and listen deeply. Without a role model, you may have learned (like me) to treat yourself the same as you were treated. For example, ignoring what you are feeling and what you most long for, or telling your child self to go away and stop bothering you.

Journaling gives you an opportunity to practice and become skilled at listening to yourself. Here are two ways to do this.

1. Free journaling means writing whatever comes out on the page, without censorship or judgment. It may be very intense, full of anger or upset, or it may be sad and punctuated with your tears. This is you being a good listener for yourself. Write by hand, dictate it into your phone, or make a journal file on your computer. All of these formats can work.

2. The non-dominant hand writing will help you get acquainted with parts of yourself. Lucia Capacchione developed this journaling practice, and teaches it in *The Recovery of Your Inner Child* and *The Power of Your Other Hand.*

Directions for non-dominant hand journaling

Take a notebook and pose a question to a part of you. Use your dominant hand, the one you usually write with, to ask your question. Then put your pen, pencil, or marker in your other hand and let that part of you respond. Continue to alternate, asking your questions with your dominant hand and answering with your non-dominant hand. The writing may look like that of a young child. That's the way it looks for almost everyone.

Some starter questions:

- *Dear Little* _____ (your name or your nickname from childhood),
- *How are you feeling today?* (Put your pen in your other hand and see what your little one has to say.)

- Then ask with your dominant hand: *what do you need from me right now to feel better?* (Put your pen in your other hand and let that little one write their response.)
- *What specific actions can I take that will help you feel safe and loved?* (With your other hand, jot down what your little one says.)

If you don't have a clear sense of actions you can take, ask some more questions of that part of you to clarify what you can do. For example:

- *How old are you?*
- *What name do you like to be called?*
- *How do you help me in my life?*
- *What do you like to do for fun?*

Notice how *you* are responding inside to these questions:

- Do you like this part of you?
- Do you ever talk to this part of you?
- Do you listen to this part of you?
- What feelings and memories are coming to mind in connection with this part?
- How does your body respond to this part?
- What does this part of you need from you right now?
- What would this part like to hear from your best self? (Your best self is that part of you that cares, listens, admits when they make mistakes or act badly, and continues to love and support your little self, no matter what is happening.)

Sometimes you won't know what to say. When that happens, write "I don't know what to say." Often, beginning to write will open the conversation. Writing in this way will feel different from how you usually write, when you know what you are going to say before you begin a sentence.

This is one way to really listen to other parts of you. It might be the first time you have listened to them. You may recognize that the only conversation you have had with the younger parts of yourself has been when you tell them how badly they messed up or how stupid they are.

These parts of you may be scared to talk to you. They may not believe that you are for real or genuinely want to listen. You may need to build some trust with them before they open up to you, just like when you meet a shy or traumatized child. You get to choose how you want to continue your relationship with them now that you know a little more about their existence and how things are for them.

Writing from one hand to another is also a way to talk with God, with people who have died, and with people who might not give you a straight answer if you asked them directly.

After you have done some journaling, the next step is to re-flect on your experience. This allows you to practice stepping back from your feelings and gives you a distinct perspective. Then you can also notice how you are feeling (your body and all the parts of you), and make some choices about the usefulness of this exercise for your growth and well-being.

Questions for reflection
1. What did you notice occurring in your body as you connected with a younger part of you?
2. What was it like writing back and forth with a part of you?
3. Were you surprised by any of the answers that came back to you?

Possibilities for your future self
1. What parts of you do you notice showing up each day?
2. Would you be willing to become more skillful at acknowledging them, their feelings, and their needs?
3. Do you talk differently to the parts you like vs. the parts you don't like? Is there anything you would like to change about that?
4. What do you believe about the parts of you? Do you think they are good or bad? Do you think they have positive intentions, or not?
5. How could you build time into your days to connect with these parts? Examples: Consciously imagine them going with you when you drive somewhere; checking in with them before you check your texts or emails; choosing to play something they like to play before you play games on your phone.

Why it's important to be aware of your pain
When my marriage ended without my agreement, I felt powerless. I had lost a sense of my own identity. Who was I since I wasn't a wife anymore? It seemed clear that communication in my marriage had failed. The underlying problem was that I had

little or no communication with myself, that part of me deep inside who had been hiding behind a submissive wifely mask.

The most I could figure out at that time was that my life was in chaos. All the rugs had been pulled out from under me. My self-confidence had disappeared into a hole. "Minus seventeen on a scale of one to ten" was the best way I could express it. Nothing felt safe, secure, or like something I could count on. And now it was all up to me. I realized in lots of ways I couldn't count on me.

The level of pain I was experiencing was excruciating. I couldn't ignore it. I couldn't go on, getting through the days, caring for four small children, without finding some ways to live differently.

I wanted to skip the pain and just jump to my personal breakthrough, but I discovered there isn't a shortcut like that. I couldn't learn "different" without examining how I had been doing things up until then. Listening to my pain was the way I first began getting up close and personal with my younger self, the self I had covered up since I was small.

Emergency Rx: If you need one simple thing to do with your pain right now, I invite you to say to yourself, as many times as you need to: *All I have to do right now is breathe.* Continue to notice each breath as you take it, and notice what shifts in your body.

This book is designed as a roadmap, to help you move from where you are to where you want to be. Now that you are aware of how pain may be showing up in your body, mind, and spirit, we will be looking at getting you the help you deserve.

Snow Heart—Ellen H. Saul © 2009

STEP TWO

Get some help for support and change

When I was four years old, I remember thinking to myself, "I'm on my own." Whatever problems came up, I believed I needed to figure them out by myself. Whatever I felt, I needed to suck it up. Whatever I wanted, I had to try to get it for myself or give up on having it.

None of that worked well, but those thoughts went along with multiple negative conclusions I had about myself. Example: *I don't matter, nobody cares, I'm not loveable, there's nothing of value about me.* These were some of the unconscious boundary beliefs that informed my decisions during the first thirty years of my life.

You deserve to have help and support as you create new healthy boundaries. I'm glad you have picked up my book, and I'm here to guide you on this journey.

My Experience Buying Gum

When I was about four years old, a day came when I *really* wanted some gum. No one in my family chewed gum, and I knew if I asked for some, I probably wouldn't get any. If my parents did agree, it would only be with reluctance, since "wants" were not considered valid in my family. Only needs like food, clothing, and shelter were important to meet.

I didn't want a handout. I had 38¢ in my blue plastic purse, and I was expecting to buy the gum. That afternoon I walked a half block to Valley Road and crossed it. It was a main thoroughfare, and I was not supposed to cross it alone. I knew how to get to King's Supermarket so that's where I headed.

All I wanted was a 5¢ pack of gum. I wandered around looking for a candy rack with single packs of gum, but I couldn't find one. All I could find was a package with ten packs of gum in it. I knew if I asked anyone for help, they would say, "Where's your mother, little girl?" So I bought one of the ten-packs. Later I realized I had spent my prized Canadian penny.

Leaving the store, I opened the first pack and put several pieces in my mouth. I walked home, enjoying the sweetness of the gum and my satisfaction over my accomplishment.

When I got home, my mother's first question was, "Where did you get that gum?" I probably lied and told her my friend gave it to me. I wasn't dumb. I knew I was in trouble. My mother finally got the story out of me and sent me to my room. At suppertime, I had to stay there. Someone brought me a bowl of bread and milk for supper. I don't remember my mom or dad talking to me about what I had done. I also don't remember any sense of being cleared of my "sin" even though the next morning I joined the family for breakfast without a comment from anyone.

Boundary beliefs about getting help

It probably isn't surprising that asking for help was problematic for me. The grownups around me didn't seem to ask for help from each other. I didn't hear them offering me help. I don't remember hearing words of affirmation or support for me or my siblings, either. My parents didn't tell me that they were proud of me, or mention what they noticed about me that they liked.

I did see my parents asking for help from God. They took time every morning to listen for God's directions for the day, their relationships, and making a difference in the world. God seemed very distant to me. I longed for the personal connections of a smile, a hug, or an offer of "How can I help?"

Why should I think about asking for help? I knew I should be able to do everything myself, and I was a pretty self-sufficient kid. Yet in certain ways, I didn't know how to even begin taking care of myself.

You may have grown up with some similar early boundary beliefs about asking for help. Some common boundary beliefs are:

- *It's not safe to ask for help.*
- *Even if I ask, I won't get it.*
- *I'll just do it myself. It will be easier than asking for help.*
- *It will only be done "right" if I do it.*
- *Shame on me if I have to ask for help.*
- *I should be able to do it all myself.*

- *There's something wrong with me if I have to ask for help.*
- *I can't admit I need help.*
- *Asking for help shows weakness, and that's* bad.

These beliefs can create a lot of negative feelings: low self-esteem and shame, for example. And some of them are simply untrue: *I should be able to do it all myself.* Says who? How can I know how to do things I've never been taught?

Here is a new boundary belief I created:
Asking for help is a gift and a blessing to the one I ask. Just as it feels good to me to help someone, I can give them a chance to feel good when I ask for help. Doing something together builds good energy for both of us. Human beings are wired to be connected. Asking for help is a wonderful way to connect with another human. I don't have to do it all alone anymore.

When I began asking for help as an adult, I faced situations where the other person said "No" to my request. Part of me could have taken this personally, but before long, I realized I appreciated their response. Instead of feeling hurt or angry, I could acknowledge their decision: "Thanks for being clear with me. I support you taking care of yourself."

I learned that it worked better if I made it safe for the person to say "Yes" *or* "No." How could I trust that their "Yes" really meant "Yes" if I wasn't sure they could say "No" when they needed to? I began to frame my request like this: "Would you be willing to help me with this project? Either yes or no is a great answer. I support you taking care of yourself here." If they said no, I knew I could figure out another way to get some help.

One reason we adults wind up with difficulties creating clear boundaries has to do with the fact that our boundaries were violated as children. A parent might say something like this: "You don't hate your brother; you *love* your brother." That's a boundary violation. Someone made a statement about how you felt as if they knew everything about you.

You didn't feel loving then, but an adult insisted they knew how you felt better than you did. This can be very confusing, and you may get into the habit of doubting yourself. *"Maybe they are right. Maybe I don't know how I feel. Maybe there's something wrong with how I am feeling."*

Perhaps your grandma died, or your favorite pet ran away, and you were hurting. In my family, people rarely spoke about sadness or even asked how I was doing. Were your feelings acknowledged as you were growing up? Were there people around who helped you name your emotions? Did you ever feel overwhelmed about what was going on? Did anyone talk with you about what had happened, and let you know your feelings were normal? How about helping you make sense of your experiences? When children don't get help with processing intense feelings, they often assume that "There's something wrong with me."

Receiving help from a safe person who can hear and acknowledge your feelings can give you a repair experience. Instead of the old memories of struggling along on your own, you feel connected and affirmed. You also have a model for learning how to speak differently to yourself. Then you can create new boundary beliefs and repair experiences for yourself. Receiving support from a safe person can help you create boundaries that keep you safe, clear, and moving forward.

When I'm feeling physical pain, I know what I can do to feel better. If I have a headache, I take an aspirin. If my back is hurting, I make an appointment with my chiropractor. If I'm sick and not getting better, I see my doctor.

I have an old boundary belief, though, that can get in the way of taking care of myself. *"It's not that bad. I'll just ignore it and maybe it will go away."*

For example, after I had fallen on the ice, my pattern was to get right up and say, "I'm okay." I quickly reassured those around me about my well-being. I was disconnected from how my body felt. My body was not "okay."

What I've learned to do is stay still and focus on my body sensations. I take the time I need to reconnect with my body. I tune into myself internally and listen for my body's message that it is ready to get up. Then I get ice or heat for the part of my body that needs it and decide if I need a higher level of care.

My new boundary belief goes like this: *My body knows a lot about how to heal itself. I can take time to be still, breathe, and pay attention to what is happening in my body. My body will let me know when it is ready for me to get up and move on.*

When you feel emotionally upset, your limbic system is fired up. That's the primitive part of your brain that processes emotions. Emotional states that can come up include anger, sadness, happiness, shame, and fear. How do you automatically respond to emotions? Maybe you experience emotional flooding. Maybe you find yourself freezing and shutting down. The practice of Mindfulness can give you structure for just noticing the emotions and letting them flow on by. Or maybe you have learned to grab your journal and start writing, a practice that can help you acknowledge those feelings and process them.

How other people are "doing" boundaries

Sometimes other people have taught us to do things that they do well. Sometimes they have taught us things that are not skillful, and the result is painful. We recognize we want to act differently. We get to think about the situation, and we can choose the actions that work for us.

While I was growing up, I often thought about how my parents communicated. Here's what I told myself: *"When I'm an adult, I'm not going to sound like my parents!"*

When I became a parent, I decided on some specific new boundary beliefs:

- I'm going to say yes as much as I can to my kids' requests: "Let's see how we can make that work," instead of "no" or a "maybe" which could turn into a "no" through inaction.
- I'm going to communicate positive energy to them: "Good job! You rock! I love you! Look at you! You can do it! I have confidence in you!"
- I'm going to show I'm delighted with who they are every day, instead of only acknowledging them when they accomplish something.

Other boundary resources

If you are working on your boundaries, you will find resources all around you. It helps to let people you trust know about your efforts. Some will share their own boundary challenges and successes with you.

The first step to healthy boundaries is to recognize when you're experiencing pain, something that isn't working well, or something that just feels off. Brené Brown, the author of *Rising Strong: How the Ability to Reset Transforms the Way We Live, Love, Parent, and Lead*, has this to say: "When we deny our stories, they define us. When we own our stories, we get to write a brave new ending." (Brown, 2015)

Owning your story is a challenge. Why? Because if you're going to articulate clear boundaries that work well for you, you need to take off your "Everything's okay" mask. Admitting to yourself that there are things in your life that aren't okay may feel pretty tough, but that's the path to growth. It may also be a relief.

Help from safe people

Human beings are genetically designed to be connected to other people for survival. Turning to people to get help with a painful situation is actually a natural instinct. However, your internal parts may resist getting help for a variety of reasons, including these beliefs: *Nobody is there to help. When I ask for help, I'm ignored, or put down, or punished in some way. There's something wrong with me if I can't do it all by myself.*

When Neal moved out and made it clear he did not want to revive our marriage, I was in so much pain I felt a huge need to tell someone. At the same time, I was feeling shame. I believed I was a failure and a bad person because I was not enough for my husband. I wanted to hide this shameful situation from my family, one where no one else was divorced. I wanted to hide it from the world, but it seemed as if everyone in my rural midwestern town knew about the affair. And part of me still believed I should manage all these intense feelings by myself.

But the part of me that didn't believe this found a couple of friends in town who listened to my story and recommended materials to read. The divorce support group I had discovered was a powerful resource. The participants in the group did not have everything figured out. Some were in as much pain as I was. They were showing up and talking about the actions they were taking. Some had even moved forward and were past the worst of their pain.

I came away from that first meeting with hope. If they could make it, so could I. I had found a sense of family in the group during this tough time. The leader of the group had completed her divorce and was now facilitating our recovery. I began to believe that there was life after divorce.

Looking back, I realize that I took steps during that time to find support for myself. Although I was a mess, something within me motivated me to get help. I began to recognize people who were helpful and others who weren't, and to make choices about how I spent my time.

Physical help

When I began to pay attention to the "things aren't okay" messages from my body, I chose some physical changes that made things better. When Neal moved out, I realized his empty seat at the table was a pain trigger for me during every meal, so I turned the table 90 degrees and put my seat in the middle of one side. Now there wasn't an empty chair at the table. I could breathe easier.

Also, climbing into a king-size bed by myself each night felt lonely and brought back bad memories of the past weeks and months. I changed the king out for a single, rearranged the furniture, and hung different pictures on the walls. The bedroom became my safe space.

Intellectual or mental help

As you read this section and the next one, you will find overlap. Mental processes and emotional processes are intertwined, and a change in either area supports changes in the other. This occurred for me when a friend suggested that I read *Telling Yourself the Truth* by William Backus and Marie Chapian. I devoured it in short order, and began recognizing the beliefs I held that weren't actually true. Those untrue beliefs led to emotions that brought me down, reactions that were hard on everybody, and behavior that was unhelpful. As I learned to identify beliefs that were true for me and establish them in my mind, my emotional state improved, and everything else got better.

Emotional help

I found a therapist who helped me learn new skills for managing my thoughts and feelings. I discovered that my feelings were intricately connected to what I believed. Then I learned that if I changed that belief, *I could change how I felt*. To this day, that is one of the most empowering things I have ever learned.

Later, I began to learn about co-dependency. I realized that my pattern of emotions had been hooked to my husband. I might have had a good day when things were going well with our kids, but if Neal came home in a bad mood, my good feelings evaporated as his black cloud expanded through the house. Nothing I did seemed to make things better. If he was up, I was up. If he was down, I was down.

A friend introduced me to Al-Anon, a 12-Step group for friends and families of alcoholics. In my Al-Anon group, people shared their stories. They helped me sort out what I had control over and what I didn't. I began to connect the Higher Power they talked about with the spiritual connections that were growing in me. I learned to ease up on expecting myself to be in control of everything around me.

Although Neal was not a drinker, my pattern of codependency was similar to the pattern of people with alcoholics in their circles. My belief about who I was depended on what Neal and others thought about me. I began to be able to separate who I was from other people and their opinions of me.

Spiritual help

In my family, my parents practiced a daily ritual of quiet time, when they listened for God's direction for their day. At breakfast everyone had the chance to share their thoughts. One person might share an apology they felt they needed to make to repair a bump in a relationship. Another might have an idea about connecting with some friends for a family cook-out. One Saturday morning my dad suggested that we all go to the beach. That was great!

My own spiritual path included numerous "shoulds" and negative beliefs. Example: *I should be connected to God, but I'm not feeling it. I should follow God's ideas for me even though I'm sure they exclude fun and what I want. I think God is always judging me negatively.*

I had little or no experience of an actual connection or relationship to God, Goddess, the Universe, Higher Power, Great Spirit. When I was about thirty, I had begun to feel an emptiness inside. I wondered, "Is this all there is?" and I sensed that this feeling had something to do with God. One day, I issued a challenge. "Okay, God, if you're there, here I am."

These are the thoughts that I received:

I'm here. If you pray, I will answer. The answer may not be what you are wanting.

That began my actual relationship with God. I spent time reading the Bible and other spiritual books. I listened for inspiration and understanding. I journaled a lot. I was excited about this new connection with God, which felt important and alive. As my experience with spirituality changed, so did my related boundary beliefs.

I am connected with something bigger than me. God cares about me. I matter to God.

When I didn't find the support I sought at church, I knew I needed a different church home where I would be accepted. I found a church which took me in, sharing fellowship, prayers, tears, and love.

Looking back, I can see some of the decisions I made to help myself:

- In my marriage, I kept hoping things would get better, and then felt devastated when they did not. As time went on, I acknowledged that things were not good. I knew I could expect anger and disrespect from Neal, so I was not surprised anymore. If something worked out, that was great, but I certainly did not expect this.
- For years, I had listened to and believed my husband's words. I did not let myself acknowledge the contradictions between his words and his actions. I was able to stop putting up with behavior I should have called out years earlier.
- Later, I realized that I could not trust my former husband's words at all. I paid careful attention to his behavior. I also chose emotional distance, because I was not willing to make myself vulnerable to someone who was not trustworthy.

My pain let me know I had to figure out new ways to respond. I could not change him. I could only change myself. I quickly adopted effective strategies for interacting differently.

I always dreaded phone calls with Neal. His habit was to use rage to take control of the situation and of me. I remember him calling to set up a visit with the kids. As his anger rose along with his volume, I held the phone at arm's length to reduce the noise. "Why are you still on the phone with him?" a little voice in my head asked.

Soon after that, I read *The Verbally Abusive Relationship* by Patricia Evans. As I started reading, my excitement grew. Evans was talking about what I had been living with for years! She gave specific directions for responding to verbal abuse. She gave me the words I had never learned.

I could say, "Use a regular voice, or I will get off the phone." Then I waited to find out what would happen. If Neal lowered his voice, I continued the call; if he raised his voice, I hung up. Done. Wow! Did he quiet down every time? No, but I knew what to do regardless of which choice he made. Empowered? You bet! It continues to be one of the best tools in my toolbox.

Exercises for Change: Help with your pain or upset feelings
The following three exercises can help you recognize and shift out of pain. They offer ways to calm and regulate your body. Start with the one that resonates most for you: breathing to calm your nervous system; grounding to settle your feelings; tapping to shift stuck emotions.

Breathing to calm your nervous system

When your body believes there is a threat and you find yourself in fight, flight, freeze, or fawn modes, here's a way to calm your nervous system and step out of the upset or pain you are experiencing. If you're not familiar with "fawn" as a response to threat, Pete Walker first started using this concept in his book *Complex PTST: From Surviving to Thriving.* He says, "A fawn response is triggered when a person responds to threat by trying to be pleasing or helpful in order to appease and forestall an attacker." (Walker, 2013) That sounds a lot like my old boundary beliefs about being a good wife: *Be supportive and helpful. I should take care of other people.*

Directions

Breathe in for three counts, then out for six counts. As you breathe in, notice how the breath feels in your nose and then in your throat. Notice how your diaphragm moves down and your belly expands with the air. Now pause just before you begin to let that breath out. Breathe out, nice and slow. Notice how your abdomen settles and your diaphragm pulls up as the air leaves. Continue this for two minutes or more.

Slowing down your breath like this slows your heart rate down. This allows everything in your body to settle. As you pay attention to those lovely, slow breaths, you also get the benefit of mindfulness, grounding, and access to your best self.

Emergency Rx: This breathing exercise is the simplest thing you can do to help yourself when everything seems overwhelming. Repeat these long, slow breaths when anxiety starts rising, or when you realize you are struggling and need some help.

Questions for reflection
1. What did you notice in the various parts of your body as you continued to do the slow breathing?
2. What happened to your emotions?
3. What is going on in your thoughts?
4. What's the state of your heart and soul as you complete this exercise?

Possibilities for your future self
1. Would you be willing to give yourself the gift of conscious, slow breathing on a regular basis?
2. What are times and places where you could build this breathing into your day? For example, before you shift from one task to another, before you drive off in your car/as you sit down on a bus or train/set off for a walk, when you notice you are no longer calm and peaceful, or during a conversation before you jump in to respond.

Exercise for Change: Grounding yourself for self-regulation
Grounding yourself involves bringing yourself into the present moment and using your senses to help you stay there. It's a way to move yourself through difficult feelings, so you can make a good decision about what to do next.

If you feel tears welling up, know that you are connecting inside with experiences from the past. Times when you weren't loved and respected. Times when people who should have kept you safe hurt you instead. Times when your heart ached and there was no one to help you feel better, or times when you felt lonely and believed that you were all alone.

Maybe you feel a flood of anger or a tsunami of rage rising up. If you are around other people, letting out that emotion can create quite a mess, which will require a lot of relational clean-up. It won't create safety for you or for them. It helped me to recognize that my brain can't be in the past, remembering pain or upset that has happened, and in the present moment at the same time.

When emotions come up, sometimes it's a good thing to acknowledge the pain, express your feelings, and allow quiet okay-ness to settle in. Sometimes, however, the time and place are not safe for you to process your emotions in this way. If so, you can choose behaviors that keep you in the present and allow that past pain to move away from you for the time being.

Directions

Imagine for a moment one of those times in your life when feelings became overwhelming inside you. It may be a recent memory, or it may go back to when you were very young. On a scale of 1-10, how big does it feel? Now slowly take a breath in through your nose. Here you will use the same kind of breaths you practiced in the previous exercise when you were breathing to calm your nervous system—long, slow breaths that go down into your abdomen.

As you continue to breathe, take a moment to look around. Name the things you can see around you. If you are indoors, you might see a chair, a painting on the wall, or books on the shelf. Naming these will ground you and help you be present in this moment in this place.

What do you hear? How many distinct noises are you noticing? Are there any smells you can identify? Where are they coming from? What can your body feel at this moment? The floor under your feet? The chair which is holding you? Your clothes on your body?

Questions for reflection

1. Take a moment to be here now. What do you notice occurring in your body? What is happening to those feelings that had been coming up? What is your level of emotion now? Remember, you have chosen to consciously place yourself in this present moment, not back in the past where the emotions may still be strong.

2. Does your body feel different now than it does when you are overtaken by emotions such as sadness, anger, frustration, or shame?

3. Would your daily life work better for you if you were good at grounding yourself when your emotions threaten to overwhelm you?

If these difficult feelings come up again, you can remind yourself that emotions are sensations that happen in your body. Then notice and be curious about those sensations. Is your throat tight or relaxed? What does it feel like in your gut? On the surface of your skin? What colors go with the sensations you are noticing? What would it feel like if you touched that sensation with your finger: smooth, prickly, textured? What's happening now inside? What has changed since you began noticing? Could you spend time there for a bit?

If you are aware of fear coming up in your body, you can continue to breathe, riding that fear through to a calmer place. Fear and excitement both come from dopamine production in your body. If you remember to keep your attention on your deep breaths, you may find the fear lessening, and you might even experience some excitement about the process.

Here's how Gay Hendricks describes this intervention in his book *The Big Leap*:

> There's only one way to get through the fog of fear, and that's to transform it into the clarity of exhilaration. . . the very same mechanisms that produce excitement also produce fear, and any fear can be transformed into excitement by breathing fully with it. On the other hand, excitement turns into fear quickly if you hold your breath. . . the best advice I can give you is to take big, easy breaths when you feel fear. Feel the fear instead of pretending it's not there. Celebrate it with a big breath, just the way you'd celebrate your birthday by taking a big breath and blowing out all the candles on your cake. (Hendricks, 2009)

Possibilities for your future self

1. As you think about your day before you go to sleep, you can practice grounding yourself in your mind. If you had an experience which didn't work so well for you, imagine a do-over. Going through the steps of choosing new responses and feeling the difference allows your brain to build some new pathways. It only takes 30-60 seconds of the newly imagined experience for your brain to change.

2. How might your life be different if you learned to respond effectively by grounding yourself?

3. How could the skill of grounding yourself change things in your relationships with family, friends, and coworkers?

4. Would the benefits for you be worth some practice and skill-building so you can better ground yourself in the face of emotional flooding?

In his book *Mindsight,* Daniel Siegel describes life as flowing down a river. When you are in the center of the river, you flow along smoothly. If you get too close to one of the banks, you can get caught up in chaos or overrun by emotions. Grounding skills are useful for shifting yourself back into the flow of the river. (Siegel, 2010)

Exercise for Change: Tapping - Emotional Freedom Technique
Tapping, which was developed by Gary Craig and first referred to as the Emotional Freedom Technique (EFT), is sometimes described as acupuncture without the needles. It provides a way to

shift emotions, energy, or physical reactions that we may experience as stuck inside our bodies.

This technique involves tapping on a series of acupressure points while using a statement about what is stuck and what you want to affirm: "Even though I'm feeling upset, I deeply and completely accept myself." Or "Even though I'm anxious about giving a speech, I choose to be calm and confident."

Directions

I have laid out a simplified version of tapping here, most closely following Patricia Carrington's Choices Method. (Carrington, 2006)

1. **Name an old experience** that still grabs your gut when you're reminded of it. Examples: *My car accident, my hospital stay, giving a speech, the scary dog.*

   _____

2. **Think of a word to name the worst feeling** from your old experience. Examples: *This fear, this pain, this anxiety.* Write it down, along with the size of this emotion as you feel it now, from 1 (low) to 10 (highest).
   This_____ _____/10

3. **Create your set-up statement:** Even though I have this_____ (fear, pain, anxiety), I choose to_____ (love and accept myself, be calm and confident, etc.)

4. **Say your statement three times** while tapping with two or more fingers on the karate chop point. You will find its location on the diagram following these instructions.

5. **Tap one circuit of the points shown on the diagram that follows.** This circuit acknowledges what you are feeling with the old experience. **As you tap on each point,** use the words in the first half of your set-up statement in step 3: "This _____."

6. **Tap a second circuit to acknowledge how you want things to be different.** Use the second half of your set-up statement in step 3 as you tap on each point. For example, "I deeply and completely accept myself." Or "I choose to feel calm and confident."

7. **Tap a third circuit alternating the two parts of your statement.** Start with the first part of your statement on the first tapping point. Then use the second part of your statement on the second tapping point. Continue alternating through the tapping points, and finish with the second part of your statement, even if you need to do another point a second time.

8. **Take a breath in and then let it out.** Notice how big your upset is now and jot it down: ____/10. If you are still significantly upset, do another set of circuits. I often do one set of circuits and then continue with my day's activities.

A few minutes later, I will discover that my feelings and my body have shifted, and I can move on.

Tapping Points

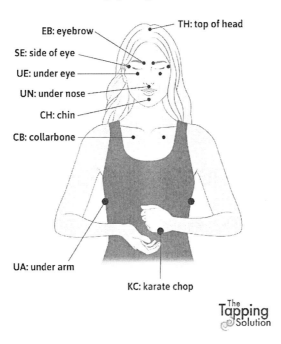

Diagram used with permission from:
https://www.thetappingsolution.com/tapping-101/#points

Nick Ortner of https://www.thetappingsolution.com/ says "try it on everything." The Tapping Solution has an app which guides you through tapping by giving you the words and the tapping points as you listen. You will find variations on tapping as you explore more. Tapping is not a precise science, so don't worry if you don't do it perfectly. It can even work when you don't believe it will!

Questions for reflection
1. What differences do you notice in your body when you finish tapping?
2. What does your body tell you about tapping? Useful? Not useful? Something else?

Possibilities for your future self
1. Could you practice tapping on a regular basis, so you are more likely to remember to use this resource when difficult feelings arise?
2. What physical, intellectual, emotional, and spiritual/energy disruptions would you like to address with tapping?

Knowing several ways to get to a calm and centered place can provide you with a foundation from which you can consider your thoughts and experiences from an adult perspective. You will have an opportunity in ensuing chapters to identify the boundary beliefs connected to your patterns of automatic responses. Once you have done so, you have a starting point for consciously choosing to keep those boundary beliefs, or updating them to match your values and your spirit.

Misty Maples—Ellen H. Saul © 2012

STEP THREE

Identify your current boundary beliefs

This is an essential step. If you don't know what boundary beliefs or rules you're operating under, it's hard to develop some new ones that will work better. In this chapter, I will help you recognize your current boundary beliefs. Sometimes they will simply pop into your head, and other times, your body's discomfort or agitation will be the first indicator that you are living with a boundary belief that doesn't fit for you. Whether you work from your body up or from your brain down, learning to notice each of your boundary beliefs is a skill that will stand you in good stead from now on.

Sometimes boundary beliefs can crop up in unexpected parts of our lives. Have you ever heard the old story about cutting off the end of the ham before cooking it? How did that get to be a practice? A woman explained that she cut the end off because her mother always does that. When she asked her mother why she cooked the ham that way, her mother said she was doing it the same way as *her* mother. When they asked the grandmother about this, she shared that she did it that way because the only pan she had for the ham was too small. Here's the old boundary belief: *I must cut off the end of the ham before I put it in the pan to cook it.* When you know where a boundary belief comes from, you can choose to keep it if that works for you, or you can update it with new information: *I only need to cut off the end of the ham if it doesn't fit in the pan.*

This next story demonstrates some of the unconscious boundary beliefs that I came up against post-divorce.

Gray Day Sundays

During the divorce, Neal and I had agreed on joint custody of our kids. For the first year and a half, visitation involved all four of the children staying with him every other weekend. Then, without warning, my ex-husband announced that starting at once, visitation would change. He explained there would be a three-week rotation. In week one, our two older children would be with him. During week two, they would come home to me, and the two younger ones would go stay with him. During week three, all four children would be with me.

We never discussed these changes. This was not a plan that took into consideration what would work best for the kids. It is a sad statement about my lack of ability to set and maintain boundaries that I only knew how to put up with this terrible situation. I don't remember even considering saying "No." Maybe I was afraid to risk further court action. I was full of fear, and my body was giving me very intense signals that this was not a good plan.

The new visitation schedule began. It seemed clear to me that my former husband wanted only two children at a time because Dawn—by now his new wife—had two children, and there was only room for two extras. The children slept as unwelcome intruders in Dawn's kids' rooms. Although Neal wanted his kids there with him in his home, between his medical practice and on-call hours, he was often gone. Two extra children created lots more work for Dawn. It was a situation designed for resentment, and the children felt they weren't wanted there.

Our four children were very close to each other, and they lost much of their connection with this visitation arrangement. Our oldest daughter, eight years old at the time, worked extremely hard trying to take care of the younger ones even when she wasn't there. She coached them about not rocking the boat, keeping everyone happy, what to do and what not to do—the same lessons I had internalized as a kid.

No one at their dad's house seemed available or capable of helping the stepsiblings connect in a positive way. The visitation schedule apparently addressed the needs of my former husband alone. This constant change and the unhappiness that resulted were overwhelming for the children. Their teachers let me know that they could tell which house the children were coming from as they entered their classrooms.

Visitation changes happened on Sunday afternoons. All day on those Sundays my body would be feeling the grief of saying goodbye. There were suitcases to pack for the week. I paid attention to clothes for activities or special events, and made sure to pack their favorite blankets. Even these were a problem since my children heard negative comments about these special belongings. I bought a second blanket for each of the children to keep at their dad's, because I couldn't trust that their special blankets would get packed to come home with them.

Gray Sunday afternoons. The stress of getting everything together and packed in the car so that we would be on time. Constantly on the verge of crying. Believing that I had to be strong to support my kids. Missing the point that this was a terrible plan and I needed to do something about it. Feeling helpless. Pushing back tears repeatedly. Having those tears well up again forty years later as I write this. So much pain. Saying goodbye in the driveway as those little ones went into a house where they received shelter and food, dislike and disgust, and little or none of the nurture and love that they needed and deserved. Then picking up the pieces of pain in the two children coming home.

Years later, these grown children shared a story about their beloved bus driver Cindy. During the time that the four of them were split up, she changed the assigned seating and allowed all of them to sit together for the ten minutes a day that they were on the same bus. It was such an important connection for them.

As the second year began, Neal told me that instead of changing homes every week, the children would stay with him for two weeks. Nothing got better. All of the children later described that time as the worst two years of their lives.

Toward the end of the second year, Neal declared that I would now have to pay for all the school lunches, even when the children were staying with him. This was not the first time he had made demands to reduce his financial obligations—not through the court, but just between us. This time I finally got it. I said "No." His reply? "See you in court." A few days later, he called me and said the visitation plan was ending. He would only be seeing the children on weekends. I couldn't believe it was over. I felt like I was waking up from a nightmare.

I still did not understand my part in this situation. I still believed my former husband had created this problem and it was his fault alone. But I was the one who had lived for two years with my body and the children's bodies in constant protest. I had continued to put up with a plan that stressed and wounded everyone.

I was living according to my old unconscious boundary beliefs:

I should keep everyone happy.

I should go along with the plan and not make waves.

I should be able to please everyone if I just keep trying.

I believed I could control what my former husband did or didn't do if I just tried hard enough. When I finally realized that wasn't happening and wasn't even possible, relief flooded through me. These were boundary beliefs that had only created pain in my life. They weren't helping me keep my children safe. These were boundary beliefs to discard.

If you have been working on creating better boundaries, you may have already discovered some of the beliefs, conscious and unconscious, that have been influencing your thoughts, feelings, actions, and spirit since you were little. As you read this chapter, you will see many other examples of boundary beliefs. What sounds familiar? We'll be working with your beliefs in the next chapter, so I invite you to start a list of them now.

Meanwhile, remember my story in Chapter Two about going to buy gum? My choices in that story were connected to my unconscious boundary beliefs, the rules that dictated how I lived and what I did. Let's look at this situation step by step.

I was four years old, and I wanted some gum. There was none in the house. As I look back now, I can state some of my boundary beliefs along with my inner conversation.

- *I'm supposed to ask for something like gum.* It won't help if I ask. If I ask Mommy, she will say "No".
- *It's too scary to ask for gum so I shouldn't ask.* Just be quiet.
- *If I hear "No" it must mean I shouldn't have asked, I don't deserve it and/or I shouldn't really want it.* But I do want it. I won't ask Mommy. I'll just go to King's Supermarket and get it.

- *I'm not supposed to cross Valley Road.* But I know how to cross the road safely. I'll just do it.
- *I'm supposed to ask if I want to go somewhere.* Mommy will say "No." I'll just sneak out.

Faced with a situation where what I wanted collided with the family rules, I unconsciously "chose" a new belief.

If I want something and I don't or won't get permission for it, do it anyway, just don't tell anyone.

This boundary belief resulted in getting the gum. It also created a pattern for me of covering up my actions. In the case of the gum, I was busted. I eventually learned to expect that whatever I hid would come out, and also learned to value waiting to act until I felt at peace with myself about those actions. As a result, I could let go of other people's reactions to my choices.

It takes some work to become aware of the early boundary beliefs by which we live. We often learn them before we have any words to articulate them. Infants begin figuring out the rules as soon as they are born. For some infants, it is enough to cry, and someone comes to take care of them. For others, nobody comes. Their boundary belief kicks in very soon: *Quit crying. It doesn't do any good. I may even get punished.*

When parents are experiencing physical or mental illness, even very young children may attempt to fill their parents' role. They may try to take care of the adults' feelings, or even try to do their parents' household tasks. When parents are emotionally absent, children may also decide, as I did, to stop trying to get their needs met at home.

Choosing new boundary beliefs

By the time I had been married seven years, I had two children under age three and a husband who was either gone at work, or home but exhausted. I baked bread for our family each week. I sewed our clothes. I was overwhelmed. What boundary belief was operating in the background?

I should do everything by hand if it is really going to count.

While we were pinching pennies on an intern's stipend, I had not really looked at any alternatives to the time and energy expenditure this involved. With two small children to care for, I had not considered how this plan was working for me. I wasn't doing well.

A friend came to visit and shared a book with me that she had been reading. Called *Values Clarification: A Handbook of Practical Strategies for Teachers and Students* (Simon et al., 1995), it contained many helpful exercises. The first one I tried suggested that I list thirty things I loved to do, and then note how often I was doing each of them. First on my list was spending time in Nature, which wasn't happening at all. I remember feeling appalled at how out-of-touch I had become from this need.

I quit baking our bread. Each morning, I would put one child in a backpack and another in the bike seat, and off we would go, breathing in the fresh air as I pedaled along the bike trail. Relief! My body let me know I was getting back on track.

Around the time of my divorce, I estimated that about 70% of my thoughts involved "shoulds." And, of course, there was the automatic push-back from my inner child, "Oh yeah? You gonna make me?" I had a lot of internal conflict. I began to work on creating new boundary beliefs that didn't use the word "should," but rather stated what I "could" do. Could is a wonderfully empowering word which gave me choices.

For a long time, if I made a mistake, I would handle it by yelling at myself in my mind: "You dummy, you shouldn't have done that, you should have known better!" I was acting according to this unrecognized boundary belief:

I deserve to be yelled at any time I make a mistake.

My new boundary belief went like this: *It's okay to make a mistake.*

My related comments to myself sounded quite different: "You could have done what you did, or you could have done something different. You caught it quickly when things didn't work well. Good for you. You know what you want to do differently for the next time. Well done! You're ready now with your better choice."

Let's look at some of the beliefs I had in my head as a child:

I'm supposed to ask for something like gum, and *I'm supposed to ask if I want to go somewhere.*

Who taught me these rules for my behavior? My parents. These were non-negotiable rules at our house. Because they were non-negotiable rules, I believed there was nothing I could do in the face of my parents' "No" except hide my rule-breaking behavior. From a parent's perspective, these were rules that made sense. From my perspective, I had to resort to sneaking around or lying to get some of my needs met.

During my marriage, I continued to believe that I had to receive permission in order to act. If I thought I would get a "No" —

or worse yet, a "NO!"—I wouldn't ask. How did this underlying belief affect me? I lived with resentment because my needs weren't met, and I thought it was my husband's fault that I couldn't ask. My body's reaction came out in eczema on my hands. At the same time, I kept the door open for doing things anyway, if I hid my behavior.

Here are some of my old boundary beliefs about asking for something.

It's not okay to ask for things. Asking for things is scary. Hearing a "No" must mean I shouldn't have asked, I don't deserve it, I shouldn't really want it, or all three. If I want something, that means I'm selfish. If someone tells me "No," it means I'm a bad person.

Your boundary beliefs come from your parents, teachers, friends, church, and culture. Some of those beliefs may have directly conflicted with other beliefs. Some of those beliefs may never have been spoken aloud. You just internalized the messages.

You may have to search deeply to articulate some of your boundary beliefs. Let's look together at several specific areas of life where boundary beliefs come into play.

Your physical boundary beliefs

Physical boundaries come to mind first for most people when we talk about boundaries. That's no surprise. We all need personal space, and we feel uncomfortable when this need isn't respected—especially when that lack of respect involves matters of sexuality.

This chapter's Exercises for Change will give you a chance to name some of the boundary beliefs that have been guiding your thoughts and actions. You can look at where they came from, notice your body's responses to them, consider how they have worked for you, and decide whether or not they are worth keeping. The following list of my early physical boundary beliefs will help you recognize some of your own.

Boundary beliefs about my body
- *I should brush my teeth twice a day.*
- *I am strong and my body can do lots of things.*
- *If my body is feeling uncomfortable, it's okay to do something to make it feel better. For example, put lotion or medicated cream on my itching hands.*
- *If my body is feeling uncomfortable with someone else's behavior, it's best not to say anything. Besides, I don't know what to say. (Certainly not "Stop!" or "No!")*

Boundary beliefs about sexuality as a child:
- *Self-pleasuring and sex are bad, so there must be something wrong with them.*
- *Flirting is bad.*
- *Having a boyfriend is very questionable.*
- *Asking questions about sex will get answers, but my mom is really uncomfortable with the whole subject.*

Boundary beliefs about sexuality as a teenager:
- *I'm not going to have sex before marriage.*
- *I'm going to experiment with behavior leading up to sex.*

Boundary beliefs about sexuality as a young adult:

- *I'm interested in sex, but I think I shouldn't be.*
- *I'm having a challenging time not feeling guilty about having sex.*
- *I'm really conflicted, and I haven't gotten settled inside myself about sex.*

What similar or different beliefs do you recall? It may be helpful to imagine going through your day and noticing the many automatic choices you make. These choices are driven by your boundary beliefs.

Let's consider three other areas of boundary beliefs that relate to the physical nature of our lives: money, time, and material objects. Again, these examples come from my own experiences growing up.

Boundary beliefs about finances:

- *My family doesn't have much money.*
- *It's important to be frugal and only buy what's useful.*
- *If you can repurpose something, that's great.*
- *I should be completely honest about money. If they give me three extra pennies in change at the store, I should return them.*

Boundary beliefs about time:

- *Work is the best use of time.*
- *Recreation should only happen when the work is done.*
- *Time just for fun isn't okay. There are too many serious things to take care of first.*

Boundary beliefs about material objects:
- *I should ask if I want to borrow something.*
- *I shouldn't steal.*

These beliefs about my physical self helped me navigate in the world. Recognizing that some of them created conflict or discomfort or real pain for me was an important step. Choosing new beliefs began to change my life.

Your emotional boundary beliefs

We acquire many kinds of emotional boundary beliefs early in our lives. Below you will find some of mine. Most of these beliefs were not conscious. They were just there, and they determined many of my choices around my emotions.

It's not safe to share what I'm feeling. I have to keep my feelings to myself.

If I share my feelings of sadness, shame, or anger, it won't go well. I'll feel sad, lonely, disappointed, or ashamed by the criticism, judgment, or discounting that I hear.

I can't trust people to treat my heart gently, so I can't share what is in my heart.

It's not okay to feel angry or to show anger. If I do, I'm a bad person.

If someone is upset with me, I must have done something wrong or bad.

I have to keep my mother from getting upset. Getting upset is too much for her.

I even had an unconscious boundary belief that directed me to avoid difficult feelings, and a whole list of things I did to keep from feeling those emotions: get a snack, get lost in a good book, clean up the kitchen, or read a magazine. (Nowadays, the list might include playing a game or two on the phone or checking Facebook.)

Each of these actions allowed me to avoid difficult feelings. They also let me ignore my child parts and what they needed. Nothing got resolved. My feelings built up. It wasn't working well for me, but I wasn't conscious enough to do much about it for a long time.

Your intellectual boundary beliefs

What are intellectual or thinking boundary beliefs? They have to do with thoughts, stories, conclusions, intentions. The human brain makes it possible for you to make sense of things that have happened in your life. You create a story about events that have taken place, and draw conclusions about what you or others said and did. You also form intentions for similar situations in the future. These cognitive processes can be disrupted by unconscious boundary beliefs.

Here are some examples of intellectual or cognitive boundary beliefs from my childhood that I had to work to find words for, because I didn't have any words for them when I was young. I just felt inner directives I couldn't ignore:

Other people know me better than I do. I had better believe them, rather than believing myself.

I should wait until others speak. I will be safer if I respond to them instead of voicing my ideas first.

I can't count on support for my ideas from my family.

When I have a plan, it will work best if I just move ahead without sharing it with other people.

If other people don't approve of my plans, that means there's something wrong with me. I'm stupid, bad, selfish, or impure.

If you are happy with me, my life is good. If you are unhappy with me, my life is bad.

There are only two judgments for things. They are either good or bad. There aren't any other ways of looking at them.

If I make a mistake, it's a disaster.

I can't show my feelings. It won't go well if I do.

Each person's experiences and thought processes are unique, yet we humans often assume we know what's going on in someone else's mind. This is hardly ever true. Even twins who are in the same situation will have a different story to tell about it. It's important to recognize that just as we don't know what's best for other people, they don't know what's best for us. You are your own expert, and you are the only person who can truly change your life.

Your spiritual, religious, and energy boundary beliefs

These types of beliefs help you consider and connect with Spirit, God, Goddess, Allah, Buddha, the Great Spirit, your Higher Power, or the Universe. In addition, let's include your own spirit energy and that of other people.

Your spiritual boundary beliefs may include specifics such as *I am a Catholic,* or *I am an agnostic,* or *I believe in the Great Spirit.*

In your adult life, you might have developed a spiritual/religious boundary belief such as this:

Each person has the right to their own beliefs and can worship accordingly.

Your childhood spiritual boundary beliefs might also include one like this:

I'm too much for my mother/father.

If your energy was quite different from theirs, they may not have known how to accept and support your energy expression.

Each one of us has a unique way of expressing our energy, yet we also share a certain set of characteristics with other people. In Carol Tuttle's book *The Child Whisperer,* she identifies four specific energy types. Type One people have upward-moving energy. They have lots of new ideas and an outgoing approach to life. Type Two folks have grounded energy. They are sensitive and very aware of the details. Type Three folks' energy goes straight ahead. They act quickly and get things done. Type Four people have centered and reflective energy. They have clear ideas for improving a plan or project. Interested in finding out your energy type? Go to www.thechildwhisperer.com. Follow the link for Dressing Your Truth/Free Beginners Guide. Enjoy this way of understanding your own energy and that of others.

You may have had to hide your energy or pretend to have a different kind of energy to get along in your family. Discovering your energy type can be a wonderful way of reconnecting to your energy and celebrating who you are. It can also help you change your boundary beliefs about how you live in the world and respond to people who have a different type of energy.

Examples of spiritual, religious, and energy boundary beliefs from my childhood:

God is keeping an eye on me to catch anything I do wrong.

I should respect all religions and people's differing religious practices.

God can talk to us, and we can talk to God.

My spirit seems to be "too much" a lot of the time. I should keep a lid on it.

You might remember a time when you were in "high spirits." It may have been yesterday or years ago. It could have been an important event, or just a great summer's day when you got to play in the water for as long as you wanted. Your spirit self was full, your spiritual energy boundaries were expansive, and you felt whole.

There may be other times you can remember when your spirit seemed dampened or even crushed. If you knew you would get a negative response, you probably didn't share your thoughts and feelings. Your essence, the most real part of you, shrank down for safety.

There also may have been a part of you that rejoiced in your spirit and felt connected to, loved by, and accepted by a higher power. For me, connecting in a positive way with a higher power has required paying attention to the boundary beliefs that I absorbed as a child, and a willingness to change many of them. I had to let in the possibility that Spirit was more than the judge I had experienced as a child.

Welcome Home

I married again ten years after my divorce. When my husband was diagnosed with Hepatitis C, his chemotherapy lasted for a year. He would get a shot every three days, and each time, this left him feeling like he had a new case of the flu. He was cranky most of the time, and ran out of energy quickly. We had to create new patterns for doing chores, and new ways to share responsibilities.

Five months into his chemo, I felt drained of both energy and patience. I found myself writing "I need more time outdoors" in my journal. Yeah, right! It was December. I went to work in the dark, I came home in the dark. How was I supposed to find time to be outdoors? A quiet thought entered my mind. "You could sleep outdoors on the deck."

In Minnesota in December? Okay, I'll try it out. The first night, layered against the cold, I took my minus-twenty-degree sleeping bag out on the deck. My breath made clouds as I wriggled into it. Zipping up, I lay back and looked up at the stars peeking through the empty branches of the oak tree. Into my mind came these words: "Welcome home!" Tears welled up in my eyes. All of a sudden, the weight of the previous months was no longer just mine. I was being held.

I slept outdoors at least one night a month for the next six months, until the mosquitos drove me back inside. My husband finished his chemotherapy, his body clear of

Hepatitis C. I still feel welcomed home every time I look up at the night sky.

Remember when I quit baking bread and took time to be out-doors instead? I still hadn't recognized that ongoing need in my life, and now I had ignored it again. The stress had become over-whelming. As I slept outdoors under the stars, actively meeting some of my needs instead of spending all of my energy meeting everyone else's, my body let me know I was back on track.

Exercise for Change: Identify your current boundary beliefs
Consider writing down one or more of your boundary beliefs in each of these areas, especially if this is a conflicted subject for you.

Directions
Sit for a moment with each boundary belief and tap into your somatic knowing. How does your body respond to this boundary belief? Is your body giving you a yes? Write a + (plus) after the belief. Are you feeling a no? Some kind of upset or tightness in your body? Mark it with a – (minus). If your body is giving you mixed signals or you're just not sure, mark the belief with a ? (question mark). You will refer back to this list in Chapter Four when we work on fully assessing these boundary beliefs, and in Chapter Five when we begin creating new boundary beliefs or tweaking the old ones.

     a. Physical
     b. Sexual
     c. Financial

d. Material objects

e. Time

f. Emotional

g. Intellectual/Cognitive

h. Spiritual/Religious/Energetic

i. Family

j. Occupation

k. Culture

l. Political

Are you struggling to identify those beliefs? Allow yourself to float back in time, into your awareness of an experience which was significant, challenging, troubling, or traumatic. One effective way to begin is to write about this experience. Alternatively, you can ask the part of you that had the experience what they believed at the time. The practice of journaling from one hand to the other (see Chapter One) might be helpful here, too. You may discover contradictory beliefs and realize that you are trying to follow both of them, even though that's impossible. That can be another indicator that some boundary belief revision is in order.

Questions for reflection

1. How old is this boundary belief? What part of you has it? (Your toddler self, your pre-school self, your grade school self, your teenage self.)

2. Do the different parts of you have any other information to give you about where this boundary belief came from? What do they want you to know?

Possibilities for your future self

1. Notice when you are in a boundary situation: holding your own boundaries, someone intruding on your boundaries, breaking someone else's boundaries. How is your body responding? Relaxed or stiff, heart pounding or calm, breath shallow or deep, throat constricted or open?

2. If you are not in a relaxed state, notice what your boundary belief is and write it down. Your body is letting you know this boundary belief isn't working for you.

3. Make a commitment to work on changing this boundary belief.

Emergency Rx: Choose just one situation that is painful or difficult for you. Identify the boundary belief that results in you repeating the same painful behavior, or getting the same upsetting result. Write down the belief that directs your choices in that situation.

As you think about the boundary beliefs with which you have grown up, you may realize that you have already changed or discarded some of them, based on your more recent experiences. You may also notice other beliefs that aren't working well, and realize that your pain is connected with the need to change old patterns and behavior. Your boundary beliefs direct your choices, whether you are aware of them or not.

In the next chapter, we will venture further into the work of assessing your boundary beliefs. During this part of the seven-step process from pain to power, you will learn how to receive the messages your pain is trying to communicate.

Calcinatio—Ellen H. Saul © 2001

STEP FOUR

Assess your boundary beliefs and keep or update

One way you can figure out whether you want to keep or change a boundary belief is to notice the effect it has on you and your body when you say it to yourself. Example: *You should always do things perfectly*. Does your body perk up, or slump? Do you feel good when you "should" on yourself? This is a boundary belief that you will probably want to change. Sometimes the need for change is immediately clear, as the following story illustrates.

Losing My Cool with My Kids

One of my most memorable experiences as a young mother occurred when my daughter was three and her brother was one. On a bright, fall morning we were getting ready for the drive to preschool. Breakfast was over, and I was running late.

I asked my daughter to put on her jacket and she continued to turn the pages of her book. Suddenly I was furious, screaming at both of them. It almost felt as if I was watching the whole scene while I was screaming.

Even as I yelled, I was appalled at myself. I knew this was not how I wanted to treat my kids. My best self, the good-enough parent part of me, knew they needed to be protected from my behavior. I silently promised them and myself this would not happen again, and as we set off for preschool, my mind was racing.

My best self wasn't a screamer, so if she wasn't screaming, then who was? I knew I had to figure that out, or the same thing was going to happen again. I thought about the situation as I drove the few miles and dropped off my daughter.

I realized that the part of me that yelled was reacting to the fifth difficult thing that had happened that morning. I had ignored the first four, swallowing my growing anger. Finally, the Screamer part of me just took over. She was fed up with the situations my adult self wasn't taking care of, and she was over the top with frustration. She was looking at the situation and saying to herself, "Ellen isn't taking care of any of this, so I have to!" That is when I had the out-of-body experience of watching myself yell.

Suddenly it was clear. The eight-year-old part of me was the Screamer. I couldn't settle myself down. I needed Big Ellen to help, and she wasn't doing that, so I could only scream.

I realized then that the frustration of my eight-year-old self could let me know right away when things were out of order in my adult life. I also acknowledged that I often didn't listen to her and didn't help her. My usual automatic response was to stop listening, turn away, and tell her I was busy and had no time for her.

If things were going to change, I would have to start listening to her. I wanted to learn to respond to my child self with compassion, to reassure her that I was there and would help her get back to a calm place.

I felt fairly confident that I could learn to listen. I knew the grownups I lived with as a child did not know how to acknowledge my feelings. I had made a promise to myself: "When I have kids, I'm going to listen when they are upset, offer them lots of love and reassurance, and be with them and help them settle down." Much of the time I was able to do that with the two little ones I had then.

When the Screamer emerged, I realized that I had learned to respond to the child parts of me just as my parents had responded to me when I was young. I was doing exactly what gave me so much pain as a child. I knew I wanted to treat Little Me differently. My relationship with myself became more conscious that day. With awareness came the possibility of change. I knew I could make different choices from there on for Little Me, and my life could be different.

Why was this incident so significant for me? I knew that I had a choice. I could make changes, or I could continue to live by my old boundary beliefs:

Ignore my upsets. It's not safe to talk about them.
I should be able to manage all the negative things around me.
It's not okay to take care of myself. My job is to take care of others.

As I began to work on my boundary beliefs, I put together three questions to help me sort out which boundary beliefs were working for me, and which ones weren't.

1. Is it true for me?
2. Does it make me feel good?
3. Does it work well in my life?

Let's check out the answers to these questions as they connect to one of the boundary beliefs identified above:

Ignore my upsets. It's not safe to talk about them.

Is it true for me? Am I in physical danger if I talk about things that upset me? No. I might be uncomfortable talking about them, but uncomfortable is not unsafe.

Does it make me feel good? No, every time I ignore what is upsetting to me, it stays in my body, accumulating negative energy. My spirit is unsettled. I lose my calm.

Does it work well in my life? No, the result of following this boundary belief is exactly what happened that morning when my kids were just being themselves and I started yelling at them.

When I considered making different choices about the boundary beliefs I used in my life, I felt empowered. I wasn't stuck with rules made by other people. I could figure out what worked for me and what did not.

Some of my experiences as a child provided me with useful boundary beliefs. For example, my dad had a workshop in our basement. I loved spending time with him there, learning to plan a project, measure, hammer, and saw. Dad's tools each had a place and I learned where they all went.

Dad's Tool Cabinet—Ellen H. Saul © 1997

Learning to Use a Spoke Shave

One day when I was spending time with my dad, he got down his spoke shave. It was a sharp blade with a handle on each end, and we used it to shave off long strips of wood.

He told me a story about being in his dad's workshop. His dad showed him where the spoke shave was kept and said, "It's really sharp. Don't touch the blade." My dad, feeling curious, waited for his next chance to take down the spoke shave. He ran his thumb along the blade and discovered just how sharp it was as the blade sliced into his thumb.

After he shared this story with me, we looked at the spoke shave and he showed me how to safely test the blade for sharpness. He demonstrated by gently running his thumb across the blade. He empowered me with a skill I have used many times since that day.

The boundary belief I learned that day went something like this: *It will work out better for me if I do things in a safe way.*

Besides acquiring a useful and effective boundary belief, I learned something about the difference between saying, "Don't do it!" and saying, "This is how to do it." That is a good example of my dad teaching me boundaries in a positive and supportive way. He knew me well enough to know that I, too, would have climbed up to test the spoke shave for myself.

Exercises for Change: Keep, tweak, or toss a belief
You will know whether it will work best for you to continue reading, and then assess your boundary beliefs at the end of the book, or take the time to do this exercise now. I know how easy it is for me to just read a self-help book, and then not come back to immerse myself in the exercises. If it feels overwhelming to look at several of your boundary beliefs, you could choose just one that seems to carry a lot of charge for you, and work on that one as you continue to read.

What you need to begin
Willingness is especially important. Sometimes I've been willing to make changes because things were so uncomfortable, I didn't

think I could stand it. Sometimes I've been willing to make changes because I felt so empty or disconnected from myself that anything would feel better than that.

You may have a sense that you are not sure who you are, or what you are here on this earth to do, or if you matter. In my experience, that disconnection goes back to our early experiences and the boundary beliefs or conclusions we made about our-selves back then. When our caretakers aren't connected to their own best selves, they don't know how to show up and be present with us, or mirror for us who we are. Then we don't have a chance to get connected to ourselves.

Our parents may see in us only the parts of themselves they reject, or the roles they assigned to us, instead of the individuals we are. As little ones, we have no way to sort out our parents' baggage from our own sense of self. We conclude that the nega-tive energy coming at us is the truth about us, and it negatively affects who we feel we are. We continue to believe that until we gain a new perspective or discover a new boundary belief to guide us.

These days, I am usually aware of upset feelings, and I take some time to sort out what's going on and what I want to do about it. Sometimes, though, I miss the fact that an uncomforta-ble situation could be just what I need to change my boundary belief and shift to another way of being in the world that's better for me.

So what else do you need besides willingness to get going? Be willing to feel the tough feelings. That is how your body gives you directions about how to move forward. You *will* get to the other side of those emotions, and you will find that your emptiness and disconnection is transforming into inner wholeness and connection.

Exercise for Change: Sway test

The sway test was developed by George J. Goodheart, Jr. A form of muscle testing used in applied kinesiology, it's a primary way of accessing your body's information and wisdom. A sway test provides a clear answer from your body, and avoids the confused thinking that often goes on and on in our heads: "On the one hand, ___; on the other hand, ___." It may be the most useful tool I've found for making decisions and functioning well in my life. A sway test is grounded in your most authentic self. It can help you know who you are, and it continues to give you clear directions for moving forward.

Directions

Stand up and allow yourself to relax on your feet, rather than holding yourself stiffly in an upright position. Go barefoot or wear shoes with flat soles and place your feet no more than shoulder width apart. Cross your hands over your heart and ask your body to show you a "Yes" by swaying forward. Pause and feel your body sway forward. Ask your body to show you a "No" by swaying backward. Pause and feel your body sway backward. It may be helpful to close your eyes or let your visual focus soften as you wait for your body's response.

You can test how this is working by saying, "Yes." Pause, and in a moment or two notice your body swaying forward.

Then say, "No." Pause, and in a moment or two notice your body swaying backward.

You can also test this method by saying, "My name is (your name)." Notice your sway forward. Then test by saying "My name is (some other name)." Notice your sway backward. Your body knows what is and isn't your name.

Try another test by thinking of something that delights your soul. Imagine it right in front of you. Does your body sway toward it? This is your body saying "Yes, this is something positive for me. I am drawn toward it."

Now think of something that you strongly dislike. Imagine it is right in front of you. Notice how your body responds with a sway away from it. This is your body saying, "No, this is something negative for me. It is repelling me."

If you have a decision to make, say something like, "The best plan for me now is to (fill in your plan)." Notice the direction of your body's sway. You can confirm your body's answer by doing a sway test for the opposite statement: "The best plan for me now is to avoid (your plan)." Notice your body's sway.

If you are getting an inconclusive answer, frame the statement differently and let your body respond. If your answer to a plan is a "no," you can check out "The best plan is to do this at another time," or "The best plan is to do this with different people."

This will work better if you are hydrated. Drink some water if you are having difficulty getting a response from your body.

A sway test can be done quite inconspicuously anywhere. It can be used to tap into your body's wisdom about anything. Your body will typically be clearer than your mind when you are considering a decision.

I learned to do a sway test after my divorce when I was in a new relationship. In more than 30 years of using this decision-making style, there has not been a time when my partner and I have experienced a result that led us in a negative direction. It has helped us individually to avoid second-guessing ourselves, and as a couple to avoid second-guessing each other. It has been a big asset to our relationship.

Questions for reflection
1. What responses did you have to doing this test? (Thumbs up or down? Did a part of you enjoy this? How old is that part?)
2. Does this seem like it could be useful to you?

Possibilities for your future self
1. What are some simple things you could ask for practice purposes? What color clothes to wear today? What to eat for a meal?
2. Could a sway test be useful at work? What task to do first? Whether to do another task or take a movement break to restore your energy?
3. How could a sway test be helpful in sorting out which people are safe for you, and which ones are not?

A sway test can be a way to evaluate your boundary beliefs and find out whether your body wants you to keep a belief, throw it out, or change it in some way.

Test: "The best plan is to keep this boundary belief."

If your body says yes, it's affirming that this is a good belief to keep.

If your body says no, test: "The best plan is to discard this boundary belief."

If your body says yes, it's an opportunity to create a new boundary belief.

If your body says no, test: "The best plan is to change this boundary belief."

Exercise for Change: Assess your boundary beliefs

Pick one issue in your life that is upsetting you. Fill in the assessment worksheet found at the end of this chapter, starting with your best guess about the boundary belief underlying this issue. There is room near the bottom of the worksheet to write in a new boundary belief, or you can complete that part of the exercise when you read Chapter Five. The Notes and Celebrations section might include the situations where this new or revised boundary belief comes into play for you, where or how you learned it, and the benefits that show up as you use it in your daily life.

Questions for reflection
1. What was it like for you to fill out this assessment?
2. What did you learn about yourself?

3. Does this process feel useful to you, or are there other approaches that would work better for you? For example, if you were to choose a color to write your boundary belief in, what would that be, and what would that tell you about keeping or changing that belief? Feel free to change this assessment sheet in any way that would be helpful to you.

Possibilities for your future self
1. What parts of your body respond when a boundary belief you are using is not keeping you safe and powerful?
2. How can you get better at noticing your body's messages about your boundary beliefs?

Winding up your assessment and moving on to Step Five
If you have found a few boundary beliefs you want to change, you are in a wonderful place to begin formulating new ones. Practicing your new boundary beliefs will give you experience, skill, and energy to continue making positive life changes.

Boundary Belief Assessment

Pick one situation that is upsetting to you. Fill in the sheet, starting with your best guess about the boundary belief related to this situation. Do a sway test. Note your responses. Create a new boundary belief if needed. Check it with a sway test.

Upsetting Situation	

Current Boundary Belief	

Sway Test Response	

Body Sensations	

Is it true for me?	

Does it make me feel good?	

Does it work well in my life?	

Keep or change?	

New Boundary Belief	

Sway Test Response	

Notes & Celebrations	

Weeping Heart—Ellen H. Saul © 2001

STEP FIVE

Create and practice effective boundary beliefs

You can choose the boundary beliefs that work for you and create safety and peace in your life. You can practice them internally first.

I invite you to look at the list you made of your current boundary beliefs in Step Three, and experiment with creating some new ones. Here's an example.

Old boundary belief:

I should take care of other people. It's not okay to take care of myself.

New boundary belief:

I could notice what I need as well as what others need. I can figure out how to meet my needs, even if that simply means taking a conscious breath. Then I will be in better shape to care for others.

How does your body respond to a choice instead of a should? Working with these new boundary beliefs expands your brain pathways, creating other ways of thinking about your boundaries.

How I Learned to Manage My Thoughts

When my first marriage was ending, I was a mess! I was depressed, lonely, ashamed, and hurt. I didn't know I could separate the feelings I was having from who I was as a person. I had no idea how to change what I was feeling. I just felt stuck.

I cried every day as the waves of sadness and hurt crashed into me. Everywhere I went there were triggers. At church, I saw a couple in the pew ahead of me. The man's hand touched his wife's back as she stepped in ahead of him. I ran into someone from our group of friends who looked away and didn't speak to me. I went to a play in our small town and felt sure that everyone there knew my husband had deserted me for someone else.

I felt powerless in the swirling darkness my thoughts created: "What an idiot! You should never have married him. Why didn't you see this coming? What is wrong with you that you were attracted to him in the first place? How come you didn't do something sooner to fix this? You should have been able to make this better."

I gained some important insights when I began seeing a therapist. One of the first things I heard about was Rational Emotive Therapy (RET), developed by Albert Ellis. It is now known as Rational Emotive Behavioral Therapy (REBT) a part of Cognitive Behavioral Therapy (CBT).

Here is a short version of RET. When I tell people about it, I say it is a way to understand what has happened in our minds when we end up feeling awful about something that occurred. It looks like this: (Ellis & MacLaren, 1998)

A	B	C
Activating event: something happens	Belief: conclusion, response that I have	Consequence: feelings I experience
Example: I make a mistake	"I messed up and I shouldn't have."	I feel ashamed

When I recognize I'm having negative feelings (C), they can be the red flag that lets me know I am saying something to myself (B) that isn't even true, doesn't feel good, or will not help me in my life. Then, I can choose something different to say to myself.

Here's an example of my old way of responding to a mistake I made (B):

You dummy! I can't believe how stupid you are to have done that! You better not let anyone know what you did!

My new boundary belief (B):

Wow! You really figured out fast that your choice wasn't the best. Smart! You could do it differently next time now that you know this choice didn't work out so well!

Possible new responses:

A	B	C
Activating event/ something happens	Belief, conclusion, response that I have	Consequence/ feelings I experience
I make a mistake	"That choice didn't work out well."	Matter of fact/ neutral
	"I figured that out quickly. Smart me."	Empowered/ positive
	"I can choose a new response for next time."	Calm/confident

Whenever I thought about what happened, I practiced my new belief. Sometimes I had to stop the old thoughts by saying "Stop!" to myself. "That's the old belief. The new belief is

_____."

With consistent practice, the new response started to run through my head on its own when the situation came up.

Overview of Step Five

In Step Three, you identified the boundary beliefs you've been using so far. In Step Four, you decided which old boundaries needed an update. Step Five is about updating those beliefs and then practicing them, so they become your new belief habit.

James Clear explained how important this is in *Atomic Habits: An Easy & Proven Way to Build Good Habits & Break Bad Ones.*

> It is so easy to overestimate the importance of one defining moment and underestimate the value of making small improvements on a daily basis. . . . It is only when looking back two, five, or perhaps ten years later that the value of good habits and the cost of bad ones becomes strikingly apparent. . . A slight change in your daily habits can guide your life to a very different destination. (Clear, 2018)

Clear summarizes:
- A habit is a behavior that has been repeated enough times to become automatic.
- The ultimate purpose of habits is to solve the problems of life with as little energy and effort as possible.
- Any habit can be broken down into a feedback loop that involves four steps: cue, craving, response, and reward.
- The Four Laws of Behavior Change are a simple set of rules we can use to build better habits. They are (1) make it obvious, (2) make it attractive, (3) make it easy, and (4) make it satisfying. (Clear, 2018)

You can tune in to your body's signal (cue) that is asking for change (craving). Your new boundary belief and the actions it leads to (response) provide you with a more positive outcome (reward). As you practice, you can fine-tune your response, applying Clear's Four Laws of Behavior Change to strengthen these new habits in your boundary beliefs, your behavior choices, and your identity. Your new behavior becomes part of long-term memory, and you can do it automatically. It has become a habit.

Would you like the new behavior to be working for you automatically next week? Of course. However, I usually give myself a year for it to become automatic. In the meantime, I give myself lots of credit for each time I practice the new habit. I deserve it!

Here's one of my family's boundary beliefs that I knew I needed to change:

It's not okay to have fun.

It was okay to be serious, responsible, industrious, and conscientious; my family rarely told jokes, teased each other, or did things that would create belly-laughs. As a result, I learned to take everything people said to me seriously. I also ended up misinterpreting how people interacted with me, which could be painful.

Later in life, when I told my parents this was one of the "rules" I took in from our family, there was a silence. Then my dad said with some wonder in his voice, "That was a rule when I was growing up, too."

I realized that until I changed my boundary belief, even when some fun snuck into my life, I would experience a guilty feeling. Laughter and fun hurt no one. They create lightness and joy. Yet I was left with a sinking feeling that somehow this wasn't okay. Here's my new boundary belief:

I value fun and laughter. I can help create them in all areas of my life.

I wanted to feel less pain and more fun. If changing what I said to myself could change how I felt, I was determined to experiment and find out what I needed to do to make this happen.

I discovered it worked! Sometimes it was a challenge to find something new to say, but I kept working on this. In fact, one of my go-to affirmations became:

There's something here for me to learn and I can figure it out.

That was incredibly empowering.

Emergency Rx: Start noticing where you are "shoulding" on yourself. If there's a "should," change it to "could." Practice saying the new statement often. Pay attention to how that's working for you. Do you notice more possibilities?

"Should" implies a directive from someone or something outside of you. "Could" implies you have a choice and can follow your values.

Old boundary belief: *I should always wait to end a phone call until the other person is finished talking.*

New boundary belief: *If I'm talking to a disrespectful person on the phone, I could hang up and be respectful of myself by no longer allowing myself to be disrespected.*

Regarding respect, keep in mind that some words carry a negative connotation and energy. Learning how to say things with more neutral or positive energy is helpful. For example, some days my energy is lower than usual and it's clear my body needs some extra rest.

Old boundary belief: *I'm so lazy. I didn't get anything done to-day.*

New boundary belief: *I paid close attention to what I needed to do today to take care of myself. I gave myself extra time to rest. I'm ready now for the new day.*

I began to notice the different energy in my choice of words:

- Deliberate and thoughtful vs. slow
- High-energy vs. hyperactive
- Quick-thinking vs. impulsive

You'll know when you have found words that work for you because your body will relax with relief when you say the new boundary belief to yourself. When you check in with your body, you'll get a thumbs up and a positive sway test.

You will have a chance to rewrite the old boundary beliefs that showed up as a "no" in Chapter Four when you did your sway test. Looking at boundaries that are physical, emotional, intellectual/cognitive, and spiritual/energetic, you can practice articulating the new rules you want for your life.

You will be looking for a statement that:

- is true for you,
- feels good when you say it to yourself,
- and helps things work better in your life when you use it.

Your new physical boundary beliefs

If you are feeling overwhelmed as you begin your list of new boundaries, feel free to decide that you will only look at one area to start with. You probably already know where you are experiencing challenges.

Are there ways that you don't speak up about your personal space? How about when people touch your body? Do you feel clear and comfortable asking for what you want or don't want sexually?

How about finances? If someone asks you for a loan, are you clear about the conditions you need to make a loan? Do your "shoulds" get in the way of being clear?

What about time? When you answer a phone call, are you clear about how much time you are willing to spend on the conversation? Do you know how to make a boundary agreement at the start of the call with the person who wants your time?

Consider your possessions. If you loan someone something, are you clear about when and in what condition you need it returned? Do you know how to respond effectively to someone who hasn't respected your belongings in the past?

Any situation that involves your body, your physical space, your time, your finances, or your possessions gives you an opportunity to notice how you are feeling and choose your response. You could:

- Do nothing and perhaps feel worse.
- Make a comment without asking for anything clearly.
- State how you feel and ask the person to please stop.
- State your boundary clearly and tell the person how you will respond if the boundary violation continues.
- Follow through on your response: do what you have said you would do.

Dr. Foster Cline and Jim Fay, authors of *Parenting with Love and Logic,* call this "Making your word gold."

If pain, discomfort, or confusion are present, they indicate a call to action. There is something here for you to learn and work through.

Your new emotional boundary beliefs

When I discovered my husband was having an affair, I kept running my old boundary beliefs through my head.

He shouldn't be having an affair! I can't believe he did this to me. He makes me so sad, hurt, and angry.

Every time I thought of this, I felt angry and frustrated, because in spite of my belief, he was having an affair. I was convinced that he had created my upset. I was angry with him about that, too.

During therapy, I learned that he was not the source of my upset. Was there something different I could say to myself?

He chose to get into another relationship. I have choices now, too. I can use my energy to get clear about my next steps.

When I am feeling angry, it's a signal that boundaries are being crossed. I can figure out what boundaries I need to make now to keep myself safe. I can do this in a respectful way. I can be aware and powerful in this situation. This is a positive way to take care of myself.

Emotional boundaries are very connected with the rest of your boundaries: physical, intellectual, and spiritual/energy boundaries. Each time you clarify one boundary for yourself, other boundaries will start to get clearer.

Examples of emotional boundaries

- Old emotional boundary belief: *It's not safe to share what I'm feeling. I have to keep my emotions to myself.*
- New boundary belief: *I can share with people a little at a time until I know how they respond.*
- Old boundary belief: *If I share my feelings of sadness, shame, or anger, it won't go well. I'll feel sad, lonely, disappointed, or ashamed if I hear a negative response in return.*
- New boundary belief: *If someone is critical or shaming when I share with them, I can choose to stop sharing with them.*
- Old boundary belief: *I can't trust people to treat my heart gently.*
- New boundary belief: *I can share with folks a little at a time and notice if they are trustworthy. If not, I can stop sharing.*
- Old boundary belief: *It's not okay to feel angry or to show anger. If I do, I'm a bad person.*
- New boundary belief: *I can know when I'm feeling angry, and I can express it in a firm and respectful way.*
- Old boundary belief: *If someone is upset with me, I must have done something wrong or bad.*
- New boundary belief: *If someone is upset with me, they are responsible for their own feelings. If they want me to do something differently, they can ask me respectfully and we can work it out.*

Your new intellectual boundary beliefs

As you consider new thinking boundary beliefs you want for yourself, look at the intellectual boundaries you wrote down in

Step Three. Is there one that brings up an emotional charge for you? Start with that and try out some new beliefs.

- Old boundary belief: *I should wait until others voice their ideas. I will be safer if I respond to them instead of voicing my ideas first.*
- New boundary belief: *I could wait until others speak, and I may choose to when I know the other person has a hard time speaking up. I could choose to speak first and be clear about my thoughts/wishes for the topic at hand.*
- Old boundary belief: *I will only be safe if I wait to respond. It's dangerous to speak up first with my ideas.*
- New boundary belief: *My safety doesn't depend on my trying to control the situation. I can remain in a discussion that feels respectful and safe or choose to take a break if it isn't feeling respectful and safe.*

Now I'm able to check if my new boundary belief meets my three criteria. Yes, this new boundary belief is true for me. When I state this boundary belief, I feel strong, safe, and empowered. It works better in my life since it directs me to effective choices, regardless of the way the other person responds. When I run a sway test on this belief, I get a sway forward, a definite "yes."

This boundary belief also challenges me to figure out what I want, and to give myself permission to want it and to speak it. Does that work well for me? Yes, I've been using this new belief in the past couple of years. When I'm clear, everyone I interact with is clearer, too. The outcome is smoother—no more of "Whatever YOU want," and "No, whatever YOU want."

It can be challenging to imagine creating a new belief, so if it isn't feeling easy, give yourself a break. This is a new skill you are learning. You can do it. Like learning to move around as a toddler, forward motion is often slow at the start.

Your new spiritual, religious, and energy boundary beliefs

Did your parents ever tell you to settle down or hurry up? Do you remember how that felt? These are comments that carry with them a message that your energy is somehow wrong or bad. Boundaries are broken when someone judges how another person feels or thinks, or who they are. In *The Verbally Abusive Relationship*, Patricia Evans identifies this as a form of verbal abuse. This boundary violation results in pain.

You may be able to remember clearly when the energy of the big people around you didn't match yours, and they didn't connect well with you. Have your spiritual boundaries allowed you to accept your own energy in a loving and compassionate way? How is it going with the people in your life? Maybe pretty easy with some people and harder with others?

Here's your chance to look back at the spiritual/religious/energy boundary beliefs you wrote down in Chapter 3. Is there one that brings up some emotion for you? That one probably needs a rewrite. Here are some of mine.

- Old spiritual boundary belief: *My spirit seems to be "too much" a lot of the time. I should put a lid on it.*
- New spiritual boundary belief: *My spirit and my energy are exactly what I'm supposed to have and what the world needs. I can celebrate and appreciate my big spirit, and at the same time*

be aware of others' spirits. They don't need me to overwhelm them.

Checking in, this feels true for me. I feel calm and joyful when I say this to myself. This works well for me. I have a way to be me and move forward.

I can choose to pay attention to the spirits of other people, to attune to them, and meet them where they are. That's important, because sometimes my big spirit comes out with lots of enthusiasm for the topic of conversation, or the ideas I have, or things I feel strongly about. I can go on and on about something.

If I'm not paying attention to the other person's energy, if I'm not listening to what they are saying, or especially what they are not saying, I can miss connections with them. I won't be effective at showing up in our relationship. I'll just show up on my soapbox, which is an extremely limited space.

As you identify spiritual/religious/energy boundary beliefs from your life so far, it may help you to notice what beliefs you have created to make safety for your spirit self/energetic self.

Change process for new boundary beliefs

I practiced my new boundary beliefs, first inside myself and later in my relationships. My process of change follows.

- The old way of doing it: Something happened that felt upsetting or off to me. I noticed, then went unconscious about it. In other words, I went ahead as if things were okay, but my body knew they weren't.
- First step of change: Something upsetting happened. I noticed, then went unconscious about it. Two weeks later, I

remembered it and realized that I felt hurt, angry, or some other feeling when it happened.

- Next step of change: Something upsetting happened. I noticed, then went unconscious about it. Two weeks later, I remembered it and realized what I felt when it happened. I figured out how I wanted to handle it another time and practiced that aloud for myself.
- The next time it happened, it only took a week to realize what happened and practice my new responses.
- The next time it happened, I realized what happened immediately after. I congratulated myself for tuning into my feelings so quickly, and I practiced my new responses.
- The next time it happened, I realized what was happening in the moment, but I couldn't quite get out the new responses.
- When it happened again, I found myself responding the way I had planned and practiced. Hooray! The situation turned out differently.

Exercise for Change: Establish your new boundary beliefs

You've worked on choosing several new boundary beliefs. How are you going to get them to stick and show up when you need them? This exercise can make it happen.

Directions

Think of a specific boundary belief that runs in your head and creates distress for you. It could be the one from your Boundary Belief Assessment sheets that comes up the most often or has the biggest negative effect on you. It's the low-hanging fruit, and it's the easiest to reach.

If I make a mistake, it's a disaster.

If you haven't yet written a **new boundary belief**, choose something different to say to yourself that would feel better. It may help if you think about what you would say to a friend or a child. Write that statement down.

I can make a mistake and still be okay.

Then listen—a part of you may argue back in response. Write that down.

But what if someone finds out?

Then write your new statement again.

I can make a mistake and still be okay.

Then write down the next response that comes back to you.

But I should do it right.

Continue back and forth.

I can make a mistake and still be okay.

I can't let anybody know.

I can make a mistake and still be okay.

Somebody will get mad.

I can make a mistake and still be okay.

I should be able to do it with no mistakes.

I can make a mistake and still be okay.
Well, people do make mistakes.

Do you notice how that comeback feels a little lighter, more neutral?

I can make a mistake and still be okay.
(No response from my brain; silent acceptance.)

I can make a mistake and still be okay.
I have made mistakes and I've survived so far.

Now you are getting a positive response. It is the third response from your brain that is neutral or positive, or a silent acceptance. This is enough writing for today. Tomorrow, do the same exercise, until you have at least three neutral or positive responses. Continue this exercise for twenty-one days, or until the new statement becomes automatic when you make a mistake.

By doing this exercise, you not only establish the new boundary belief you want, but you also start clearing out all the related thoughts that have helped support the old belief. It's as if you are replacing broken bricks in a wall. Each negative thought you acknowledge gets replaced with the new boundary belief that will work better for you.

Here's what goes through my mind now when I realize I've made a mistake:

"Wow, Ellen, you realized really quickly that was a mistake! How do you want to handle it differently next time? Got that clear? Great! On to the next thing. Nice job!"

The new words bring more positive feelings. My body feels better. I feel empowered as I learn from this choice and make a different one next time. My mistakes become a way I connect with others, rather than a shameful, hidden part of me that keeps me separate.

Questions for reflection

1. How do you feel when you use your new boundary belief?
2. Are you aware of some anxiety? That's a very normal response to trying out a new behavior. It's as if a part of you believes you are breaking the rules. In a way you are. You are changing your choices from the boundary beliefs or automatic rules you learned when you were growing up, to new ones based on being aware of what's not working and how you want to do it differently.
3. How old are the parts of you who are feeling anxious?

Possibilities for your future self

1. How will you recognize when you need to instill a new boundary belief? How can your body let you know?
2. When you are using your new boundary belief and anxiety comes up, what could you say to reassure the parts of you that are anxious? How can you remember to reassure them?

Here's a favorite poem of mine which first showed me this process of changing old boundaries to new boundaries to create a new life path.

Autobiography in Five Short Chapters
by Portia Nelson

I

I walk down the street.
There is a deep hole in the sidewalk
I fall in.
I am lost ... I am helpless.
It isn't my fault.
It takes me forever to find a way out.

II

I walk down the same street.
There is a deep hole in the sidewalk.
I pretend I don't see it.
I fall in again.
I can't believe I am in the same place
but, it isn't my fault.
It still takes a long time to get out.

III

I walk down the same street.
There is a deep hole in the sidewalk.
I see it is there.
I still fall in ... it's a habit.

My eyes are open
I know where I am.
It is my fault.
I get out immediately.

IV
I walk down the same street.
There is a deep hole in the sidewalk.
I walk around it.

V
I walk down another street.

(Nelson, 1993)

The exercise for change you practiced in this chapter is just as useful in establishing your new rules for boundaries with other people. That's what we will be working on next.

Stormy Afternoon—Ellen H. Saul © 2021

STEP SIX

Practice your new boundary beliefs with others

"People don't know what you want. It's your job to make it clear. Clarity saves relationships." (Tawwab, 2021) With this statement, Nedra Glover Tawwab identifies the purpose for making clear boundaries with others, even in the midst of the challenges that may occur.

Boundaries with others can benefit from these ground rules:

- You can change your behavior and make new choices for youself.
- You cannot change the behavior and choices of the other person.
- You can support yourself by developing boundary beliefs that keep you safe and calm.

Here's a basic boundary belief for relationships:

I deserve to be treated respectfully.

I certainly believe we do. How about this for a follow-up boundary belief:

I can be clear about when I will engage with another person and when I won't.

The Night the Shoe Brush Landed

BANG! I jumped at the noise, sensing violence. What had happened? My breath caught in my throat. Adrenaline was flooding my body. I ran to the living room where my husband had been polishing his shoes before we went out for the evening. We had been talking as we got ready for our first outing after our honeymoon. I looked around. The shoe brush lay across the room from Neal. His face was angry as he looked at me.

My thoughts immediately started racing: Why did he throw the brush? Everything seemed okay, but now he's so angry. This is awful! I can't ever let this happen again.

My mind scrambled to produce a plan for the future to prevent Neal's anger, which felt extremely dangerous to me and very scary:

- Don't make spontaneous comments.
- Don't share my ideas.
- Act quickly to prevent the anger from flaring.
- Cover up what I did, or bought, or said.
- Lie if needed.

I was locked into my early boundary beliefs: Stay safe. Don't say what you're thinking. It's not safe to be yourself with others. You can't confront anyone. There is no safe way to do that.

I knew I wanted to treat other people with respect and care. Somehow that didn't apply to how I treated myself. I didn't know how to speak gently to myself, to be supportive and to respect who I was inside. I lacked words for standing up for myself in the face of behavior that was disrespectful, abusive, or painful. I didn't yet understand that treating others with respect and care included talking about tough topics.

I never talked with Neal about that situation. I was too afraid. But our paths had started to separate. It took ten years for us to divorce.

During my relationship with Neal, I didn't know any other way to interact with him. All I knew was that sometimes things were okay between us and sometimes they were pretty awful. Things began to change when I came across Patricia Evans' book, *The Verbally Abusive Relationship: How to Recognize It and How to Respond. (2002)*

Evans explains there are two distinct power styles in relationships. One she calls Power Over, or Reality I. It kills the spirit. "Power Over shows up as control and dominance." (p. 27) In this win-lose orientation, the person who uses a Power Over style thinks there is only one truth—theirs. That's what is going on when verbal abuse occurs. Power Over is never about mutual problem-solving. It's not based on respect for the other person. It's one up, one down. Your body lets you know when you are talking to Power Over. Your body may be yelling, "Get me out of here!" even if you aren't listening to it. Your body knows the Power Over style is toxic to your spirit.

Evans continues by describing Personal Power, or Reality II. Personal Power involves a win-win approach where multiple perspectives are respected. Personal Power invites each person into their grounded, best-self space, rich with connections and calm. Your body recognizes when Personal Power is happening, and it relaxes. Each person's boundaries are being honored. Problem-solving can happen effectively.

It is common for one partner to believe that Power Over is the only way to do relationships, while the other partner believes in Personal Power, and doesn't realize that's not the case for both of them. The second person engages in genuine communications, without recognizing the control attempts of the other person. In the process, self-esteem gets demolished, because the Personal Power partner believes the negative messages of the Power Over partner.

When two people are both coming from a place of mutuality and respect, they can work out problems easily. On the other hand, if one person uses a Power Over style and the other person gives a "nice" response, two things happen. First, this sends the message that verbal abuse and control are okay. Secondly, it conveys that the "nice" partner is willing to continue an abusive relationship. When one person wins and the other person loses, the relationship loses, so ultimately both people lose.

Establishing healthy boundaries with others is an essential part of taking care of ourselves, but at times, this can be quite challenging. Let's consider some effective ways to respond to Power Over situations.

The boundary belief I have chosen for myself in relationships reflects Patricia Evans' Personal Power style:

I choose to act in a way that says, "I matter, and I know you matter, too," and I will do so to the best of my ability. When I don't succeed, or when I act as if you don't matter, I want to make things right with you, learn from what didn't work, and get clear about how I will act differently the next time.

You can practice your new boundaries with others. You can support yourself by using boundaries that keep you safe. You can decide what you will do if the person respects your boundary and what you will do and say if the person doesn't respect your boundary.

We will be looking at the four basic areas of boundaries we have addressed in earlier chapters—physical, intellectual, emotional, and spiritual/religious/energy boundaries. Your clarity about your boundaries will give structure to your interactions with others. In Step Six, the focus is on recognizing another person's Power Over reaction to a boundary you are creating, and then responding appropriately and effectively.

Practicing your physical boundaries with others

One day at work, I heard a knock at my door. A man from the next office was there with a question. Almost immediately, I began to feel uncomfortable with how close he was standing to me. I crossed my arms over my chest and stepped back. I answered his question, and he went back to his office.

I was glad I was paying attention to my body's protest at his intrusion into my personal space. I affirmed myself for using my body language to create some safety for myself. When we were talking, I didn't have any words ready to address my discomfort with him directly. It has been difficult for me to know what to say in situations like this, since I was raised to be "nice" and not to make waves. I believed that I shouldn't say anything, or I would be seen as mean, and that would be awful/emotionally dangerous/or even cause others to abandon me. That has now changed. It can for you, too.

Here are some possible responses to this situation:

- "Please step back, I'm uncomfortable with how close you are standing."
- "Hey, back up!"
- "I would appreciate your respect for my personal space."

What are your physical boundaries during a conversation? Will you continue talking to someone who yells at you, or stands over you with a dominating attitude? Are you clear about words you can say and actions you can take to respond effectively?

Emergency Rx: I have characterized Patricia Evans' response to emotional/verbal abuse/yelling like this: "Stop! Lower your voice (or change your tone) or I'm out of this conversation." Then listen to your body as the other person responds. If your body relaxes, it's okay to stay in the conversation. If your body tightens further, end your part of the conversation by leaving the room, hanging up the phone, or stopping the car and getting out. Stop responding in any way to the other person. Staying present when verbal abuse is occurring can put you in a dangerous place if the other person escalates from verbal abuse to physical abuse.

If someone is physically standing over you as a way to gain dominance in an interaction, some possible responses include standing up, moving back, or excusing yourself for a bathroom break. If you think you are in physical danger, leave the space as quickly as possible.

After you are out of the situation, give yourself credit for ending the interaction. Clarify your boundary/safety plan for the next interaction with that person. This is especially important when there is a history of physical abuse.

Practicing your intellectual boundaries with others

How do you speak up to support your new intellectual or thinking boundary beliefs? Here are some samples to consider while you choose the words that work for you.

Let's begin with a new boundary belief that you will recognize from the previous chapter.

I could *wait to speak until others speak, unless I know the other person has a hard time speaking up.* I could *choose to speak first and be clear about my thoughts about the topic. My safety doesn't depend on my trying to control the other person's behavior. I can choose to remain in a discussion that feels respectful and safe, or take a break and leave if it doesn't feel that way.*

Here are some ways to express that new belief:

"I'm going to share my ideas, and then I'd like to hear your ideas. I have confidence that we can find a solution that works for both of us."

"I would love to hear your idea about this. Then I'll share mine. We can figure this out together!"

New boundary belief: *My thoughts are valid even when others have different thoughts.*

Words to express that:

"You and I have different thoughts about that."

"I understand that's what you believe."

"Let's agree to disagree about this."

New boundary belief: *If someone tells me what I think, they are violating my boundaries. Nobody lives inside me and knows what I am thinking. I can speak up to acknowledge what just happened.*

Words to express that:

"It's interesting to hear what you think is going on in my mind."

"So *that's* what you think!" This comes across better when expressed with some genuine interest. Using sarcasm hasn't worked well for me.

As you go through the day, your body will continue to let you know if and when your boundaries are violated. Has your breathing changed? Is your stomach in knots? Do you feel angry? Do you feel cold or hot all of a sudden? These signals from your body indicate that your boundaries are at risk. Even if you don't notice these reactions in the moment, when you take some time to think about what happened, you will become more skilled at recognizing your somatic knowledge.

Practicing your emotional boundaries with others

Your new emotional boundary beliefs can include your right to have feelings and to have them respected. They may include how you choose to interact with people when you are feeling upset with them. I encourage you to continue noticing your responses to others via your body, mind, and heart. When you feel upset or activated, that's a great signal to check out the boundaries you are using. They may need some adjusting.

Here are some possible options for you to consider:

I can work problems out with others in a respectful way.

My feelings are valid for me. I can support myself and my feelings even when someone else questions or discounts my feelings.

When you create a new boundary, and the other person honors it by saying "Okay," and backing off, things shift smoothly back into a balanced interaction. Sometimes, however, the response from the other person isn't so respectful.

You should do this! Come on, everyone's doing it, it will be fun! Your friends will miss you if you aren't there!

What is your first response to this? For a long time, I didn't know how to get myself out of situations where I wanted to say "No." Maybe I gave a fake excuse, or said something like this: "My mom will kill me if I do." I didn't know how to refuse, and I was afraid of the person's reaction if I said no. You may have your own list of reasons why you have trouble saying no.

Here are some examples of effective responses in a challenging situation:

Thanks for asking; that's not going to work for me.

"Oh, come on, you can do it!"

What did you hear me say?

"That it's not going to work for you."

That's right. Thanks for understanding.

"Come on, we want you to come!"

I bet you all will have a great time, see you later. (Leave.)

Or: *I'm exhausted. I've got to take a break. You won't even want to be around me if I come! Thanks for understanding.*

When you can remind yourself of your boundary, it may help you calm down.

My job is to take care of me. If I've got some energy to spare after that, I could offer to help with the other person's needs.

Then you're in a better place to interact with the other person.

If someone is obviously upset and is coming at you verbally, you can say, "It seems like you're feeling angry. That's a bummer! Do you want to talk about what's going on?" When you reflect someone's feelings back to them and they feel heard, sometimes people can shift gears into a Personal Power style.

A follow-up option is to offer help: "Is there anything I can do to help?" It's also possible to ask a question to clarify: "I wonder if there is something that is causing a problem between us?" If the other person identifies something specific, you may be able to take responsibility for your actions, make amends, and clear up the difficulty.

If the other person's response creates tightness in your body, or some other form of somatic activation, that's an indication they are continuing in a Power Over style. It's time to make use of the Emergency Rx response and get out of the interaction.

Practicing your spiritual boundaries with others

Do you notice times in your life when your spirit feels crushed? If so, I'm glad I'm not the only one who experiences that. What to do when you hear something, and your spirit sinks? I invite you to start by connecting with your inner self. That's where the wound is.

Bridging the Gap—Ellen H. Saul © 2009

When My Spirit Sank

Near the end of a visit with my dear sister, she said something that threw me into what I call the Shame Pit, where my spirit feels crushed. She mentioned that when we talked, I offered helpful solutions all the time in response to what she was saying, even when she hadn't asked for any help.

Instead of listening deeply and affirming her feelings, I told her how to solve her problems. All my ideas, meant as gifts, had discounted her capabilities. She knows exactly what she needs to do and is very able to ask for help when she needs it. She spoke about her feelings of resistance to all my good ideas. She shared an "ah-ha" moment for herself as she recognized the difference for her between choices that she had made for herself, and "good ideas for things she *should* do" that others (I) gave her/pushed on her.

I was very aware of the gap between my intention to be present to support her, and my actual behavior, which had an ego-boosting flavor threaded through it. A wave of shame crashed over me. And even as it inundated me, a part of me knew:

This is a well-worn brain path for you. You don't have to make this all about you. You have a chance to listen now, in ways you haven't listened before. You can affirm her spirit for speaking up and for all that she is learning. You can tell her how much you love her.

On the inside, I focused on my new spiritual boundary belief:

My spirit and my energy are exactly what I'm supposed to have and what the world needs. I can celebrate and appreciate my big spirit, and at the same time be aware of others' spirits. They don't need me to overwhelm them.

Tears sprang into my eyes. I gathered up my younger self and talked just to her:

It's okay, I'm here. I love you. We do have big energy and it can overwhelm folks. We can own it and practice being in balance inside and outside with others. You're okay. I love you. We'll do it together. You can always be with me, just as you are.

With a sense of peace inside, I went to my sister and told her what had come clear to me. She thanked me and we shared a long hug. We acknowledged how much we value our ability to talk openly when something doesn't go well between us, to hear each other, and to rebuild the bridge of this relationship we both treasure.

Using your boundary beliefs with others

Have you ever found yourself complaining about a situation without getting clear what you would like instead? Does it seem like the only solution to your problem is for the other person to do something else, but they keep doing the same frustrating thing?

How fair is it if you expect the other person to do something different, but you don't? How empowered do you feel if you aren't clear about what new action you can take, especially if the other person does not change anything?

In this chapter, you will have a chance to try out a successful process for requesting a behavior change. While it may seem very structured and a bit uncomfortable at first, it has helped many folks learn the steps of successful problem-solving.

Problem-solving with someone takes two people who are willing to interact from the place of Patricia Evans' Personal Power: a belief that each person matters. Personal relationships between two people with positive intentions fit this description. Effective problem-solving works well when each person can be present as their best self.

The first part of this process makes it possible for the other person to find out where you are coming from. You share three things:

- What the problem is for you
- The emotions you are experiencing
- The thoughts which triggered those emotions

When you have expressed these things clearly and calmly, it gets a little easier for the other person to listen to your request.

The second part of the process involves letting the other person know specifically what you are asking for—the behavior change you want. And along with your request, it's only fair to state clearly what you are willing to do. So, let's try this out.

Exercises for Change: Problem-solving with others

Problem-solving between two people begins when we agree that something isn't working, and we decide to cooperate to create a possible solution. We also agree to try our solution out and, if needed, perhaps change it later.

At times in my life, full of frustration, I've tried to get someone to change their behavior by saying to them, "Quit that!" The result has usually been stubborn refusal, defensiveness, an argument, and no resolution. This is a completely different process.

The following exercise incorporates qualities of respect and balance. If you are going to ask someone to make a change, it's important to do so as calmly and kindly as you can. First let them know what's going on with you, how you're feeling and what you are thinking about the issue. When the other person knows where you're coming from, it's easier for them to feel some empathy, connection, and willingness to work together to find a solution.

Requesting a behavior change

I am including a problem-solving form here. The first page will help you prepare for the meeting you hope to have. This gives you time to reflect and settle yourself, and allows you to figure out what new behavior you want to request. Then you can begin this process as your best self, with a calm body and spirit. Also included are directions for how to go about requesting a meeting, and how you can introduce guidelines for your conversation.

The second form will help the two of you navigate your meeting in a thoughtful and caring manner. It includes the steps of the problem-solving process, with space for the thoughts you will be sharing, so you don't have to keep it all in your mind. When you meet with your friend, bring two copies of the second form with you, so you can each fill one out as you work together to complete the exercise.

Preparing to Request a Behavior Change

Think about and write down a one-sentence description of the problem you are having. Then get in touch with your friend.

Person 1 to Person 2: I realize that I'm having a problem with

_____.

Would you be willing to work with me on finding a solution?

When and where could we work on this? (Person 1 has chosen the agenda, Person 2 gets to choose the time and place.)

If the other person agrees to meet, appreciate the fact that your friend is willing to work on this issue with you. That's so much better than charging into a battle where there are no winners!

When the meeting takes place:

Person 1: I want both of us to know that we have been heard, so I will reflect back to you what I hear and check to see if I got it right. Would you be willing to do that, too?

Person 2: Yes or no. Even if they say no, you can reflect what they say during your conversation, and you can ask again if they will reflect what you say as well.

Person 1: I'm wondering if we could both fill out a copy of this problem-solving form (on the next page of this book, and available online as a PDF at https://ellensaulcom) before we take turns sharing our feelings, thoughts, and ideas for what we could each do differently. Is that okay with you? (Take time to write in silence.)

Problem-Solving Sentence Starters, Process, and Agreement

When I hear (or see) _____

_____

I make myself feel: (mad, sad, glad, afraid, ashamed, or a combination of feelings) _____

Because I think _____

What I'm willing to do is _____

What I'd like from you is _____

Decide together who will speak first. The first speaker shares their completed sentences, and the listener reflects back what they've heard, concluding with this question: "Did I hear you correctly?" The speaker can clarify if needed, and the listener can reflect again.

Switch roles and repeat the process. When each understands the other, say if you are willing to meet the other's request or offer an alternative response. Come to agreement on future action and note that, along with a date to revisit your agreement to modify it if needed. Sign and celebrate. You have a way forward together.

Agreement details:

Date to revisit agreement:

Signature: _____ Date: _____

Signature: _____ Date: _____

Questions for reflection

1. How did your body respond to doing this exercise? How did the format help you shift into your resourceful, adult self to complete the exercise with the other person?

2. What part of you filled it out? Are there child parts of you who would also like to be heard this way? Would you be willing to give them a chance to do that?

Possibilities for your future self

1. Even though you won't want to use this process for every little thing that comes up, the principle behind it may be useful for many situations. It's difficult to solve a problem if nobody makes a request. Getting clear on what you want to ask for is an important step. Letting the other person know what you are willing to do helps balance the request you are making.

   It's also hard to work something out if you don't have a specific request from the other person. If you hear a complaint from them, you can check out the items in the sentence-starter form with them.

   You may be able to guess about what's going on (1), and help the other person express the problem: "I'm guessing you're talking about yesterday when …, right?" "It sounds like you are feeling angry and frustrated. Is that what you're feeling?" (2) "I wonder if you're thinking this means I don't care about you?" (3)

   The unspoken request may be a complete mystery to you. In that case, this may help: "I'm wondering what you might want to ask for here (4), so we can solve this problem between us and clear the air." When they do make a request, see if you can say yes to the request. If you aren't feeling settled about it, you can always propose another solution, and keep working on it until you have an agreement for moving forward.

2. If someone else is upset, you can hold clear emotional boundaries by remembering they are making themselves upset. You didn't cause their feelings, and you can't make their emotions go away, because you can't change what they are saying to themselves about what happened.

   You could choose to acknowledge their upset by stating what you notice: "It sounds like you are feeling really angry," (or frustrated, or irritable, or sad, or scared). Then you can pause. That moment of acknowledgment followed by silence might be enough for the person to collect and soothe themselves, so the conversation can continue peacefully.

   If that doesn't happen, and they act more upset, you can decide what kind of physical boundaries you want. You could stay close by and let the other person's upset continue to land all over you. You also have the option to remove yourself for a time to another place where you feel safer and more peaceful.

   If you are the one who has been upset about something, your clear emotional boundaries might help you say something like this: "Wow! I sure have gotten myself amped up. I'm going to take a time out until I calm down. Then I'll come back and check in with you again."

After you're settled down, you could come back and acknowledge to your friend what happened inside you and how you're choosing to handle it now. You might also make amends if you were implying your upset was their fault.

3. If you are not making any headway toward a solution, you may be talking to someone who is more interested in Power Over than in working things out. In that case, you need to change gears and respond effectively to Power Over tactics. You might recognize that your body is feeling stressed and choose to take a break. "This doesn't seem to be helpful right now. Let's call it quits and see if we want to try again later." This allows you to leave the stress for the time being, calm yourself, and restore your equilibrium.

   Taking a break may also give you space to recognize Power Over behaviors: irritation, blaming, anger, intensity, controlling, put-downs, criticism. If these are showing up, the other person's agreement to engage in problem-solving may not be genuine. You may need to figure out how you can effectively respond to the other person's behavior without their buy-in on making changes.

Patricia Evans' research into verbal abuse brought to light the following fact: While verbal abuse doesn't always escalate to physical abuse, when physical abuse *is* present, verbal abuse has preceded it. Removing yourself from the scene of verbal abuse can be an important protection from physical abuse. Getting out of a situation like this works better if you have created clear boundaries and a plan of action that you have already prepared and rehearsed.

Many people weren't taught how to solve problems when they were children. If you grew up trying to keep the peace, you may have little experience in figuring out what you might want or need. Your boundaries may also dictate that you aren't supposed to ever ask for these things. This could be a great place to start making some changes to your early boundary beliefs. The problem-solving exercise I have presented here may be a bit easier when your new boundary belief sounds something like this:

The best plan is for me to be clear about what I want and need. I can state that clearly to the other person. I can also listen carefully to what they want and need. We can figure this out, so it works for both of us.

Exercise for Change: Practice new boundaries using your imagination

Toward the end of your day, take a bit of time to think through that day's experiences. Notice any interactions which didn't work out as well as you would have liked.

- Rerun the interaction in your imagination, taking all the time you need to figure out where things went awry.
- Notice what boundary beliefs you were using. Consider choosing a new boundary belief to use in this interaction. What is your new boundary? What are the words and actions that would go with this new boundary?
- Imagine saying and doing these things. Notice how the other person responds.

- Continue the scene in your imagination until you have a satisfactory conclusion.

This is an effective way to practice your new boundaries and improve your skills. A variation on this exercise is to role play the situation with a supportive friend or therapist. Your brain gets a chance to build new pathways that match your new boundary. If you are clear on how you want to do this in the future, it's possible to go to the other person, let them know you're unhappy with how you behaved during your end of the interaction, and ask if you could have a re-do. Then you get a chance in real life to have a different and more positive result.

Questions for Reflection
1. How did it feel to reimagine the interaction that didn't go so well?
2. How could this be useful in practicing new boundaries with yourself?

Possibilities for your future self
1. Can you create a habit of re-imagining interactions that didn't go well in real life, so you are ready for your next chance to use your boundaries effectively?
2. What are some ways you can support yourself for making these changes, or get support from others?

In this chapter, we've explored a variety of ways to practice your boundary beliefs with others. You may be overwhelmed with the scope of new behaviors that are available to you. If so, give yourself permission to start with just one thing that you are ready to change. It may be most helpful to choose something that isn't noticeably big.

As I mentioned earlier, my first change was shifting from "should" to "could" in my thinking and my speech. I received positive benefits from that change. It was more fun living in my head after that. My body relaxed more. In addition, when I stopped "shoulding" on others, my relationships smoothed out. There was less defensiveness, and more empowerment on both sides.

I encourage you to just take it step by step. Experiment with changing one old belief. Notice the effect of that one change inside and outside yourself. When you're ready, come back and re-read these steps, or you may be ready to begin changing another belief. You may discover some ideas you missed the first time, or you may be ready to begin changing another belief.

One of my new boundary beliefs here is:

Clear is better than nice.

It keeps me on track when I start to fall back into my old beliefs.

Now it's time for the final step from pain to power: celebrating who you are and how you have grown. Why is this step part of the process? Our brains are wired to look for problems and unresolved issues, things we have to notice in order to survive. We're less adept at celebrating problems we've solved, changes we've made, and how our lives are working better. That's what we'll be addressing in the next chapter—creating energy to continue positive changes.

The Light is Now—Ellen H. Saul © 2014

STEP SEVEN

Celebrate your changes and yourself

Step Seven is about discovering ways to celebrate yourself, to acknowledge your feelings, to affirm yourself. You deserve a cheer, a pat on the back, a warm smile, and words of appreciation.

Let's glance back over the past year of your life.

- What's different now from a year ago?
- What can you appreciate?
- What have you learned to do differently?
- How is that helping your life?

We notice what's wrong as a survival skill to help us stay safe and alive. Noticing what's right, what's better—that can be a "thrival" skill for our spirits. John Demartini coined this word. "Thrival" fits what we're going for here—a big step beyond survival! In his book *The Values Factor*, Demartini talks about the importance of getting clear on your own values. When you base your boundaries on your values, what you do on the outside can match what your spirit values on the inside.

During my divorce, I discovered that I was not good at cheering myself on, mainly because I had learned in my family to focus on what was wrong. In the years since then, I have learned to be a cheerleader for myself and others. It's a skill that gives me joy.

No matter what you learned or didn't learn early in your life about affirming yourself, you can now choose to get better at recognizing and celebrating your progress, your increasing skills, and your forward movement.

Emergency Rx: Think back to a time when you remember being unhappy with yourself. Now consider the situation from your current perspective. Think about what has changed since then. Notice what you *can* appreciate, even if it is merely the fact that you have survived the days since your difficult memory. Give your Little Self a smile and let them know, "Cheers for you!" Give your Adult Self a high five. Hang out with those positive feelings for 30 seconds or more, so they get activated in your brain. Sometimes nothing has changed outwardly, but gaining a new perspective on an old story can make things feel quite different.

Buying Gum: A new perspective

Remember my story in Chapter 4 about going to buy gum? That story is about how my parents parented me. As I got more connected with my Child Self, I felt the shame, loneliness, and disconnection of that 50-year-old experience. After reading Howard Glasser's *Transforming the Difficult Child: The Nurtured Heart Approach*, I thought about how differently my parents could have handled that situation had they known a better approach.

Glasser suggests parents can give reflective feedback to their children about their behavior. He uses the language of photography to explain his ideas about parenting. He defines a Kodak Moment as one when a parent describes to a child what they saw the child doing. A Polaroid response describes healthy aspects of behavior the parent wants to encourage. A Canon response is when the parent identifies the rules that the child has followed.

Changing My Old Story

As I finished reading Glasser's book, I wanted to feel what it would have been like to receive those responses in my family. I used my imagination to reenact that old scene in my head and I wrote a new ending for that story. This time when my mother saw me with my gum, she responded "Hey there, it's good to see you! You look pretty pleased with yourself. Looks like you've got some gum and it tastes good. I think you might have had an adventure. Tell me about it!" (Kodak moment)

My Child Self: She wants to hear my story! I can tell her all about it.

When I finished my story, my mother smiled and looked proud of me. She said, "You noticed what you wanted, and you did something about it. You were creative. You made a plan that was realistic and do-able. You figured it out without any help, and you followed through all the way to the end. You used your smart brain: you knew where to go, how to get there, and how to find what you were looking for. And when you got home and I gave you a time-out, you cooperated and took your time-out right away, just as I told you to." (Polaroid moment)

My Child Self: Wow! That was a lot of good stuff. I didn't even know I could do all those big things. She just kept saying more. She's proud of me!

And then my mom went on: "You paid for the gum. You looked both ways and crossed Valley Road safely. You were respectful to me when I asked you about the gum and when I gave you a time-out. Nobody got hurt in the process. You came home after you finished your mission and checked in with me. There are a lot of things you did today in just the way we have taught you. You are quite a young lady, and I love you!" (Canon moment)

My Child Self: I DO know how to do things. I am pretty grown up. Mommy is proud of me. She loves me.

Journaling about this was helpful to me in several ways. I realized how hard it was for me to name the rules I had followed, or give myself credit for that, even as I broke other rules. I want to get better at reflecting all the positives that are present in a situation, even in the midst of mistakes in judgment, or significant messes. I want to be able to use this skill generously with all the people in my life, celebrating the positive side of what is.

I was emotionally bowled over by the contrast between how this scene played out years ago and the warmth and energy of my reimagined scene. I felt a deep sadness. To shift my sadness, I took some time to process it using the tapping exercise you learned to do in Chapter Two. As I tapped and affirmed "I deeply and completely accept myself," I realized several things:

- My mother would have parented differently if she had known how. She didn't have support from people who could teach her about this, or resources (books, webinars, blogs) to learn it from. I believe it pained her, also.
- My mom hid what she felt, and I learned to do the same. I have kept an emotional distance from others much of my life because of this unhealed pain.
- As a result, I have not been ready to feel and respond to some of the hurts that others carry.
- I felt shame for the little girl I was because she didn't get what she needed and believed she couldn't get help. I have tried to cover up the shame while carrying it with me.

Using tapping, I was able to feel and process these feelings in just a few minutes. As I write this, I feel grateful for the chance to get to the other side of those difficult, stuck feelings. Looking at my story from a different angle has allowed me to create a repair experience for my Child Self. Little Ellen and I have made this story ours; she isn't going through it all alone anymore. I see her, I hear her, and I celebrate her smarts, her spunkiness, and her agency. She gets things done. She triumphed in this story and we both know it.

Here is the new boundary belief that I created:

I can tune in to my Child Self, Little Ellen, and help her when she needs and wants it. I can be clear about the people in my life that I can safely and reliably depend upon when I ask for help. I can delight in ending the story in a new way in my own mind and heart.

Overview of Step Seven

You've made it to the final step!

- You've had a chance to experience the challenge of hanging out with your body and feeling your pain. (Step One) You have decided you want to feel differently.
- You've been given some ideas for finding ways to get help and support from a safe person, a coach or therapist, and/or a helpful book like this one. (Step Two)
- You've had an opportunity to identify some of your boundary beliefs. (Step Three)
- You've learned a way to assess whether those boundary beliefs are working for you or not. (Step Four)
- You've written at least one new boundary belief that you want to incorporate into your relationship with yourself. (Step Five)
- You've had a chance to identify at least one new boundary belief you want to practice with others, and you have tried it out. (Step Six)
- Now you're here at Step Seven and we can celebrate. Look at you! You're doing this!

Celebrate your changes with yourself

Think back to the way things were before you started reading this book. What feels different now? Do any of these statements resonate with you?

I'm not so down on myself. I'm feeling a bit more hopeful. I spoke up yesterday and said, "No, I don't want to." Someone asked me for help when I was really tired and I said, "That's not going to work for me right now, but thanks for asking. Maybe tomorrow."

As you've read the stories here, you have encountered some new boundary beliefs that you may want to try out for yourself. You have considered many examples of new boundary beliefs, along with the words and actions you can use to put those boundaries into practice in your life. You know the ones for which your spirit yearns. You also know how to get started. Celebrating change has several parts:

- Recognizing changes
- Affirming yourself on the inside by affirming the parts of you
- Affirming yourself on the outside with safe, supportive people

First, let's notice and celebrate areas in your life where you've made changes. Remember the story of how I got so mad at my kids before preschool? I recognized a pattern in me and was able to identify the parts of me that were players in the scene: my Adult Self, standing on the sidelines, quite appalled at how I was acting; my 8-year-old Screamer Self who was on overload and who wasn't getting any help from me. It was clear to me that I would do a lot of damage to my kids if I continued that pattern. Several things came to mind:

- I realized this upset was the fifth one I had felt that morning, and it wasn't even 8:30 am!

- I had tried to ignore those frustrations and I got more upset.
- I realized I didn't have to avoid feeling my upset. It was just there, letting me know some part of me needed my attention and care.
- I decided I needed a plan for handling frustration and anger differently, such as saying something different about it to myself, having something different to say in response to the other person, doing something different, or all three.

  Example: *Oh, this is one of those times when I'm overwhelmed. I hate it when this happens! Let's do some jumping jacks! Or go outdoors and take some breaths. Or do a somersault.*

I made my plan, got clear on my new interpretations of what was going on, and practiced my new words and actions. I never screamed at my kids like that again. Even when I was in the middle of a marriage relationship that was challenging and painful, I was still paying attention. I knew to look for ways to make changes in me, even if I couldn't change things outside me.

I've added tools to my toolbox for the times when I begin to feel overwhelmed.

- I know now I can take some breaths, feeling them all the way in and out, and my body will calm.
- I can check inside, asking who needs some help, and listen to the upset young parts of myself. I can reassure them that I'm here, and I'll take care of the situation, so they don't have to.

- I have more words to express what's going on in me, and I can tell others what's happening without feeling ashamed and bad about myself.

These are some of the ways I've learned to be the best parent I can be to myself. I notice when I'm using these tools and I cheer myself on. It feels so much better than when I used to yell at myself all the time. I find things to celebrate every day.

Celebrate your changes with folks who affirm you

Finding supportive people is particularly important. They can confirm what you are experiencing, ground you in reality, and cheer you on with each little step. They can listen when you need to vent, especially if you have asked for that, and they say "Yes."

Look for people who embody Patricia Evans' description of Personal Power, the ones who respect themselves and you. Your body is your helper here. You will feel peaceful and calm around these folks. These are the people you can work things out with when there is a glitch in your relationship.

You might find these important people anywhere:

- Family members who "get" you, who have a shared experience and understand how you may be feeling.
- Safe friends who acknowledge what you are experiencing, affirm your feelings, ask you if you want their ideas, and don't make it all about them.
- A life coach who can share ideas, be a cheerleader for you, contribute possible ways to proceed, and pay attention to your sense of direction.

- A therapist with whom you feel emotionally safe, who has information and skills related to trauma and mind-body connections, who wants you to grow up and out-grow therapy, and who honors your dreams for the future.
- A spiritual advisor/pastor who can support you in your spiritual quest for growth and understanding.
- A support Group such as Alcoholics Anonymous, Al-Anon, Adult Children of Alcoholics/Dysfunctional Families, a divorce group, a grief group. Shop around, find one with the flavor of support that feels right to you.

Celebrating with someone might have several different looks. You will know what fits best for you!
- It could be simply having some time together to hang out.
- It could be making and keeping an appointment with a professional support person.
- It might be hanging out with a friend, visiting over coffee or a meal, working on a puzzle together, or even sitting in silence and sharing a smile.
- It might be creating a special occasion—perhaps attending a play, a class, meeting for a meal at a fancy restaurant.

Maybe one of your parts needs a celebration. Doing a little writing from one hand to the other can clear up what they need. Remember Chapter 1? Check inside and see what that part of you has to say.

Celebrating is something you can learn to do well. Practice helps.

It's okay to have fun with safe people.

How's that for a boundary belief that supports your celebrations?

Exercises for Change: Celebrations

Celebrations can be large or small. Remember a time when you saw a dear family member or friend after months or years apart? Perhaps for the first time since the Covid lockdown? Feel the joy you felt then. Remember your expression, your smile, perhaps the tears that sprang to your eyes, the delight that filled your body. That was a celebration all in itself! It's a celebration you can have any time, and you don't even have to send out party invitations.

How else can you celebrate yourself for the steps you are taking to create healthy boundaries? You can make a list of affirming phrases to say to yourself: "Great job! You rock! Look at YOU! Cheers for you!"

In *The Nurtured Heart Approach*, Howard Glasser demonstrates giving partial credit. That's where you get to appreciate yourself for each move in the direction of your new, clearer boundary beliefs.

I realized I have a boundary problem in this situation or relationship. Good for me! I've practiced my new words in front of the mirror. I've planned when I'm going to use them, so I have them ready. I'm doing it!

Another way to celebrate

Take some time, perhaps as your day is ending, to think about your day. Fill in any of the sentence starters that apply:

I survived this day by_____.

I took care of myself by _____.

I had fun with these parts of me today:_____.

I recognized a boundary issue when _____.

I used one new strategy today: _____.

I used a new/updated boundary belief and noticed how it worked out:_____.

A big thing happened today and my part in it was:_____
_____.

Give yourself a lot of credit! Look what you've noticed from just one day: all the ways you are using what you have learned to make change and move forward with your healthy boundaries. Whoop it up! Woo-hoo! Imagine all the parts of you together, surrounded by your love and compassion. Breathe in this celebration. Let the cells of your body warm with it. Let your mind, heart, and spirit take it in and smile. Give it time—thirty seconds or more—so it settles in and stays. You deserve to be celebrated!

Questions for Reflection

1. What did you experience in your body as you celebrated?
2. How did the parts of you respond to being celebrated?
3. Could each smile that crosses your face represent a celebration? How many can you notice in a day?

Possibilities for your future self

1. When you celebrate positive things in your life, by acknowledging them to yourself or others, you give them more energy in your life. What you energize shows up more often. Are you noticing the celebrations you give energy to and getting the benefit of each of them?

2. Take some time to think about your perspective on various moments in your day. An example might be the thoughts that go through my mind when it's time to take my dog for a walk. Am I running negative thoughts? "Oh no, I haven't got time for this, what a pain, I wish someone else was doing this." Or am I noticing the positives? "Here's a chance to have time with my dog, move my body, smell some fresh air, and see what Nature is up to today. I wonder what we will discover. I'm smiling—it's a celebration."

3. Seeing someone, recognizing how their best self is showing up, and naming what you are experiencing from them is a way of celebrating them.

   - You are introduced to a new baby. You welcome that baby with delight and celebration. It shows up in your smile, soft eyes, warm voice, and gentle touch.
   - Something doesn't go as well as you would like with your partner. You choose to start a conversation by expressing something that you appreciate about your partner. You choose to believe that their intentions are good.

- In the same way, noticing and listening to the different parts of you affirms who you are internally. When you celebrate yourself, you show up as the best-parent-you-can-be-to-yourself. Imagine the effect that can have.

Might there be a part of you with an empty space inside? The one that's been waiting and yearning to hear warm words and feel your delight? You can give those words and that positive energy to yourself. Celebrating you can reshape your inner landscape. I believe you can create a safe space inside where all the parts of you get to grow and play and live in delight. You have the power to do that.

Building your energy by celebrating

When I had to complete a big paper as part of a certification process, I was overwhelmed. I couldn't see a clear path from where I was to the finish line. Every time I thought about it, I felt frozen. I couldn't muster up the energy to do anything.

At that time in my life, I had some practice in looking for the boundary beliefs I might be holding unconsciously, and identifying ones that led to being stuck. Eventually I discovered what was blocking me:

I can't give myself any credit, or celebrate anything, until every iota of a project is completed.

With that old boundary belief, the long process of writing a major paper was taking lots of my energy without giving me any energy back. No wonder I felt stuck.

I wrote myself a new boundary belief:

I deserve to give myself credit for every tiny step I make in the direction of my big goal.

I also decided to make myself a Backwards Planner. First, I imagined all the work was finished, my certification had arrived in the mail, and I was opening it. Next, I imagined the last thing I would have done before that: mailing off all the final paperwork. Then I imagined the action before that: collecting the required signatures on the provided forms, and before that, receiving approval from the three readers of my final paper. I continued like this, all the way back to the point where I was writing down these steps in the Backwards Planner.

When I finished, I had a big celebration with lots of cheering for myself. I also began to share the steps I was completing with positive support people in my life. They celebrated with me, and I was energized. I didn't expend energy trying to decide what to do next, because I already knew—the bottom step on the Backwards Planner. My celebration for each step gave me the energy to take the next one.

That's why Step Seven is about celebrating. Once you notice a change you have made and celebrate it, you are creating the energy and the safe space to make the next change.

Emergency Rx: On the days when it seems there is nothing to celebrate and you need a boost, you can celebrate yourself for surviving your day. "Look at you! You're doing it!" Getting through this minute and this hour can be cause for celebration all by itself.

We're coming up on the closing chapter now. You've walked through this process with me, and you have the tools and the energy to expand what you've learned here throughout your entire life. Go for it! You can do it!

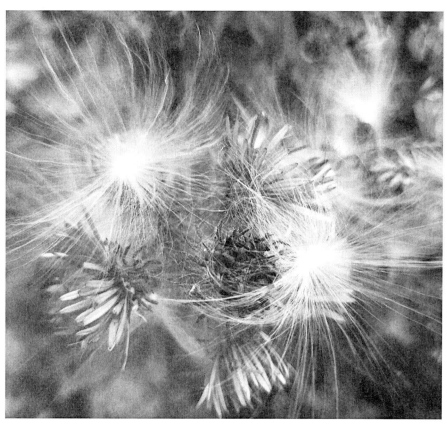

Milkweed Journey—Ellen H. Saul © 2022

TAKING THESE BOUNDARY LESSONS INTO THE WORLD

Difficulties in adulthood are often rooted in difficult experiences in childhood. Perhaps you lacked safety growing up, or the big people in your life weren't able to attune to your needs, or maybe they were dealing with physical or mental illness and that used up their attention and energy.

I'm so glad you've joined me on this life-changing journey. You have been using the Seven Steps roadmap to gain-awareness of yourself, your body, your emotions, and your beliefs. With that awareness, you have practiced tuning in to yourself in ways that may not have happened for you in childhood. You listened to and met the needs of your Child Self as you became an agent of repair. You began using these skills and your updated boundary beliefs with others in your life—friends and family members.

As you continue to create and make use of your new healthy boundaries, you will send healing ripples out into the world.

Let's review the Seven Steps once more

I'd like to walk with you through the steps one last time before you continue on your own journey. As I summarize my story of transformation, you can choose to take a little time to review and tell your own story. There is space here to write it down if you feel ready to do that.

Step One: Recognize your pain. I was overcome with sadness due to the end of my happily-ever-after dream; overcome with shame when I believed I was not good enough for my husband to want to stay married to me; and overcome with anger at the unfairness of it all.

How your pain shows up:

Step Two: Get some help for support and change. I was determined to do something. When I finally began to realize I couldn't do anything about my husband's choices, I sought out help for myself. I gathered information, and I found people who knew more than I did about getting through this painful turning point. I put together action steps as fast as I could figure them out. I kept the ones that worked and discarded those that did not.

How you are getting help:

Step Three: Identify your current boundary beliefs. My brain was yelling at me all the time: "You should…," "You shouldn't…," "You should have…" I began to name the boundary beliefs that were driving my decisions and actions. While a few of them worked, most of them caused stress and interpersonal messes.

Your boundary beliefs:

Step Four: Assess your boundary beliefs and choose to keep or update them. What a possibility! When I realized that I could change the boundary beliefs I had used my whole life, I began to feel more empowered. I knew right away which ones worked well for me. I also knew where my boundary beliefs had led me to ineffective actions, an activated nervous system, and a diminished spirit. I was willing to change those beliefs.

Boundary beliefs to keep:

Boundary beliefs to update:

Step Five: Create and practice effective new boundary beliefs within. Instead of "shoulding" on myself, I began to say,

> *You could choose to do this, or you could choose to do something else. What would work better for you?*
> *All I have to do right now is breathe.*

I found that I could settle myself more easily, even in difficult situations.

Your new boundary beliefs and how they are working for yourself:

Step Six: Practice your new boundary beliefs with others. I began to state and hold my boundaries with other people. As I practiced, I got better at it. I was learning how to keep myself safe, and I found I had fewer messes to clean up in my relationships. I felt more settled, less scared, and less overwhelmed.

Your new boundary beliefs and how they are working out with others:

Step Seven: Celebrate your changes and yourself. I wanted to keep making positive changes. I hadn't grown up surrounded by people who cheered me on, so I had to learn to celebrate myself, my new boundary beliefs, and my new actions. Some people wanted me to give in as I often did before my transformation, but I didn't let that derail me. Even if others weren't supporting my new behavior, I could notice my changes and celebrate them. I'm still celebrating!

How you are celebrating yourself:

Although I didn't learn about boundaries soon enough to make any difference in my marriage, I began to recognize Power Over when it was showing up around me. I began to fill my Seven Steps to Healthy Boundaries toolbox with effective responses, and I became a woman who doesn't take shit from anyone.

As Patricia Evans has stated, "If we are to recognize and free ourselves from the influence of the Power Over model, we must hear ourselves—what words we speak and in what manner we speak them. Likewise, we must hear the words spoken to us and the manner in which they are spoken. This awareness can bring us to the realization of how we do or do not dignify, respect, protect, and esteem ourselves and ultimately all life." (Evans, 1992)

Looking back and moving ahead

Consider how things have gone for you as you have been making changes to your boundaries. Remember the feeling you get as you speak up for yourself and state a new boundary? This is the time to breathe deeply. With full breaths, your body can register excitement. With shallow, rapid breaths, it will register fear. You deserve to be excited about making these changes.

When you are working on your boundaries, the Universe will continue to provide you with multiple opportunities to practice what you need to learn. You may notice you feel frustrated: "Why is this happening again?" Instead of repeating this old refrain, you can celebrate with a positive statement: "Yay! I have another chance to get really good at setting this boundary!"

Practical next steps of awareness

- Check in with your body throughout the day to notice what's happening with your energy, your emotions, your mood, and your thoughts.
- Listen carefully. Does a part of you need something from you?
- If so, act to meet that need.
- Connect this check-in to things you do regularly during the day: standing up or sitting down, washing your hands, scrolling on your phone.

A vision for your future

By now you've had a chance to discover and experience the consequences of the boundary beliefs you have developed so far.

You may be getting very skilled at recognizing boundary beliefs that serve you well and others that don't. I hope you have felt a change in your relationship with your Child Selves, the parts of you that have been struggling to exist in a grownup world with their child-sized awareness and limited resources. Your Child Selves deserve your support and protection. They have been doing their best. Now you have a chance to step up and become the best parent you can be for them. Use what you have learned here to help you.

I can imagine you moving forward in your life in a new way. I am confident you will find yourself making positive changes, perhaps just in your thinking at first, as you realize there are other options for you that you may not have considered before.

You will know what's right for you. You will find the help you need. And you will create a life for yourself that continues to provide you with more satisfaction, more peace, and more wholeness. I wish you all the best as you continue to use these Seven Steps to Healthy Boundaries to light up your path as you move forward in life.

ACKNOWLEDGMENTS

My deepest thanks:

To Dr. Carl "Chuck" Lofy, for helping me realize I was on the Hero's Journey, and what my next steps could be.

To my teachers, especially David Blair and Kay Smedley, and to my therapists, who taught me, who believed in me, and who loved me.

To each client whom I have been honored to work with in therapy sessions. We have shared a journey as we learned together about boundaries.

To Mary Penley, who asked me to recommend a good book on boundaries and who heard me say, "I could probably write one." That was the start of this book.

To Pat Geary, who met with me for a year as we talked through the Hero's Journey, holding space together for the seven steps that wanted to show up in this book.

To my inspired Beta readers: Alice Chaffee, Roslyn Nappa Duffy, Sarah Fisher, Sean Quinn, Eliana Papagianapolis, Connie Ryberg, Kathy Sigler, Laura Soble, Cameron Speth, and Lisa Sugarman.

To my special cheerleaders, Nancy Hawkins, Judith Morris, my Sand Sisters, my Reflective Supervision group, and my Dellwood Friends.

To Margaret Smith & Phillip Tyndale-Biscoe, Diana Raphael, and Susan Hodges & Tim Denny, who welcomed me into their homes for my writing retreat weeks.

To my Women of Words writers group, who encouraged me and shared ideas and expertise throughout this process.

To my editor, Ruth Ellen Allard, whose support and clarity helped bring this book to birth with joy.

To Trina Brunk, an inspired coach and artist who listened to my vision, looked at my artistic style, and created a book cover that delights my soul.

To Ann Aubitz of Kirk House Publishers, who met me with enthusiasm, co-operation, and creativity to bring this book into physical being.

To Little Ellen who delights and encourages me every day.

To my parents, who taught me perfectly what I came to this earth to learn.

To my former husband, who helped bring our four amazing children into this world, and who left our relationship when it was time.

To the members of my family, who have consistently supported me and cheered me on: my siblings and cousins; my kids and step-kids and their partners; my grandkids, whom I hope will live their lives with knowledge of healthy boundaries and the skills to act on them; and especially my sweetie and husband of thirty-three years, who has shown up again and again with support and encouragement, and who has let me know from the start of a very long process that I could write this book.

PERMISSIONS

Grateful acknowledgment is made to the following for permission to reprint previously published material:

Simon & Schuster: to include the poem "Autobiography in Five Short Chapters" from *There's a Hole in My Sidewalk: The Romance of Self-Discovery,* by Portia Nelson. Copyright © 1993 by Portia Nelson. Reprinted with the permission of Beyond Words/Atria Books, an Imprint of Simon & Schuster. All rights reserved.

Carl "Chuck" Lofy: to include his ideas about the Hero's Journey, shared at a workshop he presented in 1986.

Carol Tuttle: to paraphrase information about Energy Profiling from her website offerings and from *The Child Whisperer: The Ultimate Handbook for Raising Happy, Successful, and Cooperative Children,* by Carol Tuttle, © 2012.

Gay Hendricks: to include an excerpt from *The Big Leap: Conquer Your Big Fear and Take Life to the Next Level,* by Gay Hendricks, © 2009.

John Demartini: to use an excerpt from the post "How to Know if You're Making the Wisest Decision—The Demartini Show Episode 152" by John Demartini, © September 30, 2022.

Nick Ortner and The Tapping Solution.com: to include a diagram of tapping points from the website.

The Nurtured Heart Institute: to paraphrase information from *Transforming the Difficult Child: The Nurtured Heart Approach* by Howard Glasser and Jennifer Easley, © 2005.

Patricia Carrington: to include ideas from *The Power of Personal Choice: An Introduction to the EFT Choices Method* by Patricia Carrington, © 2006.

Patricia Evans: to include excerpts from *The Verbally Abusive Relationship: How to Recognize It and How to Respond* by Patricia Evans, © 1980.

Penguin Random House LLC: to include an excerpt from *Set Boundaries, Find Peace: A Guide to Reclaiming Yourself* by Nedra Glover Tawaab, © 2021.

Penguin Random House LLC: to include an excerpt from *Atomic Habits: An Easy and Proven Way to Build Good Habits and Break Bad Ones* by James Clear, © 2018.

Penguin Random House LLC: to include an excerpt from *Rising Strong: How the Ability to Reset Transforms the Way We Live, Love, Parent, and Lead* by Brené Brown, © 2015.

Pete Walker: to include an excerpt from *Complex PTSD: From Surviving to Thriving* by Pete Walker, © 2013.

Sounds True Inc: to include an excerpt from *No Bad Parts: Healing Trauma and Restoring Wholeness with the Internal Family Systems Model* by Richard Schwartz, © 2021.

BIBLIOGRAPHY

Backus, William and Marie Chapian. *Telling Yourself the Truth.* Bloomington, MN: Bethany House Publishers, 2014.

Brown, Brené. *Rising Strong: How the Ability to Reset Transforms the Way We Live, Love, Parent, and Lead.* New York: Random House, 2017.

Capacchione, Lucia. *Recovery of Your Inner Child: The Highly Acclaimed Method for Liberating Your Inner Self.* New York: Touchstone, 1991.

Carrington, Patricia, PhD. *The Power of Personal Choice: An Introduction to the EFT Choices Method.* 2006. https://patcarrington.com/the-power-of-personal-choice-in-eft/

Clear, James. *Atomic Habits: An Easy & Proven Way to Build Good Habits & Break Bad Ones.* Toronto, ON: Avery, 2018.

Craig, Gary. *The EFT Manual.* Fulton, CA: Energy Psychology Press, 2011.

Cline, Foster and Jim Fay. *Parenting with Love and Logic.* Colorado Springs, CO: NavPress Publishing, 2006.

Demartini, John. *The Values Factor: The Secret to Creating an Inspired and Fulfilling Life.* New York: Berkley Press, 2013.

Ellis, Albert and Catherine McLaren. *Rational Emotive Therapy: A Therapist's Guide.* Atascadero, CA: Impact Publishers, 1998.

Evans, Patricia. *The Verbally Abusive Relationship: How to Recognize It and How to Respond.* Stoughton, MA: Adams Media, 2010.

Glasser, Howard and Jennifer Easley. *Transforming the Difficult Child: The Nurtured Heart Approach.* Austin, TX: Nurtured Heart Publications, 1999.

Goodheart, George J. Jr. *Applied Kinesiology: The Neuro-Lymphatic Reflex and Its Relationship to Muscle Balancing.* No publisher, 1965. Out of print.

Hendricks, Gay. *The Big Leap: Conquer Your Hidden Fear and Take Life to the Next Level.* San Francisco: HarperOne, 2010.

Levine, Peter A. and Anne Frederick. *Waking the Tiger: Healing Trauma.* Berkeley, CA: North Atlantic Books, 1997.

Nelson, Portia. "My Autobiography in Five Short Chapters." *There's a Hole in My Sidewalk: The Romance of Self-Discovery.* New York: Atria Books/Beyond Words, 2012.

Ortner, Nick. *The Tapping Solution: A Revolutionary System for Stress-Free Living.* Carlsbad, CA: Hay House Inc., 2014.

Schwartz, Dr. Richard. *No Bad Parts*: *Healing Trauma and Restoring Wholeness with the Internal Family Systems Model.* Louisville, CO: Sounds True Publishing, 2021.

Sheehy, Gail. *Passages: Predictable Crises of Adult Life.* New York: Bantam Books, 1977.

Siegel, Daniel. *Mindsight: The New Science of Personal Transformation.* New York: Bantam Books, 2010.

Simon, Dr. Sidney B., Dr. Leland W. Howe, and Dr. Howard Kirschenbaum. *Values Clarification.* New York: Grand Central Publishing, 1995.

Tuttle, Carol. *The Child Whisperer: The Ultimate Handbook for Raising Happy, Successful, and Cooperative Children.* Lehi, UT: Live Your Truth Press, 2012.

Walker, Pete. *Complex PTSD: From Surviving to Thriving.* Charleston, SC: CreateSpace, 2013.

ABOUT THE AUTHOR

Ellen H. Saul is a licensed psychologist who specializes in the process of healing from trauma and attachment wounds. She has a master's degree in Community Counseling from Minnesota State University, Mankato. Her pronouns are she/her.

Ellen had four young children when her first marriage ended, and she learned the hard way that her personal boundaries weren't creating safety and confidence. Her search for effective answers and powerful action led to a life-changing inner journey, graduate school, and an ongoing commitment to helping others.

Ellen married again and during the next thirty-three years, a blended family of eight grew to twenty-six. Ellen believes the challenges of a blended family should make every year count for two! She and her husband share their southern Minnesota home and their hearts with Annie, a rescue Shepherd-Pit-Husky-Mastiff mix.

There once was a girl from New Jersey
Who feared that she just wasn't worthy.
She got stuck in the dark
Til she first saw a spark
And learned to make good topsy-turvy!

Visit the website for updates and PDFs of forms:
https://www.ellensaul.com